D0173072

OPERATION
SNOW

OPERATION
SNOW

HOW A SOVIET MOLE
IN FDR'S WHITE HOUSE
TRIGGERED PEARL HARBOR

JOHN KOSTER

REGNERY
HISTORY

Copyright © 2012 by John Koster

All rights reserved. No part of this publication may be reproduced or transmitted in any form or by any means electronic or mechanical, including photocopy, recording, or any information storage and retrieval system now known or to be invented, without permission in writing from the publisher, except by a reviewer who wishes to quote brief passages in connection with a review written for inclusion in a magazine, newspaper, website, or broadcast.

Regnery History™ is a trademark of Salem Communications Holding Corporation; Regnery® is a registered trademark of Salem Communications Holding Corporation

First paperback edition 2015: ISBN 978-1-62157-292-3
Originally published in hardcover, 2012: ISBN 978-1-59698-322-9

Library of Congress Control Number: 2014466429

Published in the United States by
Regnery History
An imprint of Regnery Publishing
A Division of Salem Media Group
300 New Jersey Ave NW
Washington, DC 20001
www.RegneryHistory.com

Manufactured in the United States of America

10 9 8 7 6 5 4 3 2 1

Books are available in quantity for promotional or premium use. For information on discounts and terms, please visit our website: www.Regnery.com.

Distributed to the trade by
Perseus Distribution
250 West 57th Street
New York, NY 10017

*To Sergeant John Cordes, United States Army Air Corps;
Petty Officer Harold Traber, United States Navy; and
Ensign Takeo Obo, Imperial Japanese Navy—the uncle
I never met, the cousin who once saved my life, and the
brother-in-law who explained the other side to me.*

CONTENTS

CAST OF CHARACTERS

Acheson, Dean. Attorney with the U.S. State Department who tightened the oil embargo on Japan beyond what FDR had intended while FDR was on vacation.

Akhmerov, Iskhak ("Bill") Abdulovich. NKVD spymaster for the United States who controlled Soviet espionage and was the controller for Vitalii Pavlov.

Bentley, Elizabeth. "The Red Spy Queen," a defector from Soviet intelligence who denounced Harry Dexter White as a Soviet agent of influence.

Berle, Adolf. Assistant secretary of state who, eighteen months before Pearl Harbor, passed a warning from Whittaker Chambers and Isaac Don Levine to FDR that Harry Dexter White was a Soviet agent. FDR dismissed the warning as nonsense.

Bykov, Boris. Soviet spymaster who served as the controller for Whittaker Chambers and later for Elizabeth Bentley, both of whom disliked him intensely.

Chambers, Whittaker. Soviet intelligence courier for Harry Dexter White. Chambers later defected and denounced White as a Soviet agent of influence. Chambers's book *Witness* provided inside details of the Soviet intelligence network in the United States.

Chiang Kai-shek. Chinese Nationalist leader and America's candidate for future control of China. He was defeated by Mao in 1949.

Christie, J. Walter. American automotive genius who designed and illegally shipped the prototype of the BT and T-34 tanks to the Soviet Union while the trade embargo was still in effect.

Currie, Lauchlin. Canadian-born economist identified by defectors as a Soviet agent in the FDR administration.

Durdin, Frank Tillman. *New York Times* correspondent who described the Japanese massacres at Nanking as factual but on a vastly smaller scale than reported in the West by historian Iris Chang.

Fish, Hamilton. Republican member of Congress from Dutchess County, New York (FDR's home district), who opposed American entry into World War II before Pearl Harbor and urged action to save European Jews. Fish was an early advocate of Pearl Harbor conspiracy.

Fumiko Hayashi. Japanese "woman's author" famous for her Bohemian lifestyle who reported Japanese atrocities during the China Incident.

Fumimaro Konoye. Japanese prince, diplomat, and prime minister on the eve of the Pearl Harbor attack. Roosevelt rejected his proposal for a last-minute face-to-face meeting to avert war.

Gardner, Meredith. U.S. code-breaker who deciphered the Soviet code revealing that the Soviet agent "Jurist" was Harry Dexter White.

Gaston, Herbert. Assistant secretary of the Treasury in charge of department security. Harry Dexter White used Gaston to approve the hiring of suspected communists in the Treasury Department.

Gillette, Guy. Democratic senator from Iowa who attempted to win a hearing for Kilsoo Haan's warnings about an impending Japanese attack on Pearl Harbor.

Grew, Joseph C. U.S. ambassador to Japan and advocate of Japanese-U.S. friendship. Grew issued several warnings about worsening diplomatic relations and a probable attack against Pearl Harbor.

Haan, Kilsoo. Korean nationalist working in the United States who, relying on reports from Hawaii, tried to warn the U.S. government that an attack on Pearl Harbor was planned for the first weekend in December 1941.

Hideki Tojo. Japanese general and prime minister (1941–1944); hanged for war crimes, 1948.

Hiss, Alger. U.S. State Department lawyer active in Soviet espionage. Convicted of perjury in 1950 on the testimony of Whittaker Chambers and served four years in prison.

Hornbeck, Stanley K. State Department expert on China who hated Japan. Neither a communist or sympathizer, Hornbeck believed that all Asians, including the Japanese, were easily intimidated, and he encouraged a tough stance before Pearl Harbor.

Hull, Cordell. Secretary of state 1933–1944; opposed U.S. intervention in Sino-Japanese conflicts and in the early stages of World War II.

Ikki Kita. Japanese folk-Christian leader who inspired the young officers of the uprising of February 26, 1936.

Iwane Matsui. Commander of Japanese forces in the Second Sino-Japanese War. Hanged for war crimes in 1948, though his personal responsibility for the "Rape of Nanking" is disputed.

Kantaro Suzuki. Grand chamberlain of Japan who survived an assassination attempt in the February 26, 1936, uprising; later prime minister.

Katz, Joseph. "First line" recruiter of Soviet agents in the United States.

Keisuke Okada. Japanese prime minister who narrowly escaped assassination in the February 26, 1936, uprising.

Kichisaburo Nomura. Japanese admiral, diplomat, and ambassador to the U.S. 1940–1942.

Kimmel, Husband E. Replaced Admiral James Richardson as commander in chief of the Pacific Fleet in February 1941. Removed of command after the attack on Pearl Harbor.

Knox, Frank. Secretary of the Navy at the time of Pearl Harbor. After ignoring warnings of a probable attack from Admiral Richardson, Admiral Kimmel, and Kilsoo Haan, Knox circulated unfounded rumors of wholesale Japanese-American espionage and sabotage as factors in the Pearl Harbor catastrophe.

Koki Hirota. Japanese working-class politician and diplomat ("the man in the ordinary suit"). As prime minister, he entered the Anti-Comintern Pact of alliances against the Soviet Union. Though hanged for war crimes in 1948, he is widely viewed as a scapegoat.

Levine, Isaac Don. Jewish anti-communist who tried to help Whittaker Chambers convince Assistant Secretary of State Adolf Berle that Harry Dexter White was a Soviet agent.

Makoto Saito. Japanese lord privy seal assassinated in the uprising of February 26, 1936.

Marshall, George. U.S. Army chief of staff 1939–1945; later secretary of defense and state.

Masaharu Homma. Japanese general who drove MacArthur from the Philippines in 1942. His execution for complicity in the Bataan Death March surprised American witnesses, who thought the evidence exculpated him.

Matsuo Kinoaki. Mysterious author of *The Three-Power Alliance and the United States–Japanese War*, variously described as a military intelligence officer and a publicist.

Mitchell, Jonathan. Speechwriter for Treasury Secretary Morgenthau who testified against Harry Dexter White before the House Un-American Activities Committee.

Morgenthau, Henry, Jr. Secretary of the Treasury 1934–1945, mentor of Harry Dexter White, and close friend of FDR.

Mundt, Karl. Republican congressman from South Dakota (and future senator) and member of the House Un-American Activities Committee who questioned Harry Dexter White in 1948.

Nobuaki Makino. Advisor to Hirohito who narrowly escaped being assassinated in the uprising of February 26, 1936.

Pal, Radhabinod. Indian jurist and member of the Tokyo war crimes tribunal who voted for acquittal on the grounds that the U.S. had provoked war with Japan.

Pavlov, Vitalii. Soviet NKVD operative in the United States who directed Harry Dexter White to foment hostilities between the U.S. and Japan.

Perlo, Victor. Communist economist who held Treasury Department and other government positions throughout the Roosevelt administration; alleged Soviet agent.

Popov, Dusko. Double agent for Nazi Germany and for Britain who offered the FBI detailed information about German interest in Pearl Harbor.

Poyntz, Juliet Stuart. American communist whose protest against Stalin's mass murders probably provoked her murder in 1938. Her fate prompted Whittaker Chambers to abandon his role as a Soviet agent.

Richardson, James O. Commander in chief of the Pacific Fleet who was ordered to move the fleet to Pearl Harbor. He warned about the Navy's lack of preparation for a Japanese attack and was relieved of command in February 1941.

Silvermaster, Nathan Gregory. Ringleader of Soviet agents (the Silvermaster group) in the Roosevelt administration.

Stark, Harold. Chief of U.S. Naval Operations at the time of Pearl Harbor.

Stimson, Henry. Secretary of war 1911–1913, 1940–1945; secretary of state 1929–1933; opposed the "Morgenthau Plan" for the de-industrialization of postwar Germany.

Stripling, Robert E. Chief investigator of the House Un-American Activities Committee at the time of Harry Dexter White's appearance before the committee.

Thomas, J. Parnell. Chairman of the House Un-American Activities Committee when Harry Dexter White appeared before it.

Togo Tanaka. Japanese-American journalist who disputed Kilsoo Haan's reports of subversive Japanese activities in the U.S. Not to be confused with Japanese foreign minister Shigenori Togo, or Gi'ichi Tanaka, Japanese prime minister.

Tsuyoshi Inukai. Prime minister of Japan, assassinated in 1932 by nationalist military officers.

Ullman, William L. Treasury and War Department official, delegate to Bretton Woods Conference, and photographer for the Silvermaster group of Soviet agents.

Yosuke Matsuoka. U.S.-educated Japanese foreign minister 1940–1941.

Zhukov, Georgi. Soviet general in the 1939 Nomonhan Incident in Mongolia.

INTRODUCTION

Why another book about Pearl Harbor? Obviously, because none of the other books got it right. I started my adult reading with *Day of Infamy* by Walter Lord—at the end of his life, Walter was a cherished friend of the family—and I would not presume to rival his mastery of what the attack looked like to the people who were there. After that, it all kind of went downhill.

Day of Infamy came out in 1957—the version I first read as a teenager was serialized in *Life* magazine when it was still a weekly. My senior cousin, Harold Traber, fought the Japanese off Saipan, in the Philippines, and at Okinawa; a kamikaze once slammed into a compartment where he had been sleeping a couple days before.

He saw the mass suicides of Japanese settlers on Saipan and wept at the sight of dead women and children floating in the water. He survived the killer typhoon that capsized three destroyers just like his own. He also saw a Japanese pilot from a shot-down plane pull a pistol and try to shoot it out with his own Fletcher-class destroyer. His ship depth-charged a Japanese submarine and got an oil slick but no bodies or wreckage and no confirmation. Hank was on the third ship into Tokyo Bay, the USS *Cushing*. He later splurged on the whole series of official books about the history of the U.S. Navy in World War II and on the comprehensive books about U.S. destroyer and submarine operations in World War II by Theodore Roscoe.

Another senior cousin, John Cordes, was killed in a B-17 bomber over Germany. His daughter grew up without a father because her mother never remarried. My own father served thirty months in the infantry. He left the U.S. Army a buck sergeant with double lobar pneumonia, a mild limp, and a medical discharge. Uncle Al Phillips, Uncle Dan Bravman, and Uncle Herb Pooley also served in World War II. None of what any of them told me bore the slightest resemblance to the "official version." I watched *Victory at Sea* by Richard Hanser and Henry Salomon, with that magnificent Wagnerian music by Richard Rodgers and Robert Russell Bennett, every Saturday night, right before my weekly bath. I learned to love thematic music and became a very imperfect Wagnerite, but as I read more, things got worse.

My father, though he was a U.S. veteran and a third-generation American, was fully bilingual—trilingual in a sense, since he had picked up German from his grandmother and the handyman, and neighborhood Italian by osmosis—and we had some interesting guests for Thanksgiving dinners: a Polish countess who had been dispossessed by the Soviets and raped by Russian soldiers in Berlin; the daughter of a German physician, once engaged to a Jewish man, later married to a World War I sniper; a Hungarian conscript who had been captured in the Ukraine with twenty-five of his buddies and was one of two who survived the Gulag in Siberia; Russians whose kids I met in college and who prided themselves on having soldiered for the Wehrmacht; any number of Germans I met in the skilled trades who had beat it out of Prussia or Saxony one jump ahead of the Red Army; Frenchmen who had been in the Resistance and Englishmen who had been in the London fire brigade or the RAF and who told me that, in retrospect, the war was not exactly as depicted in textbooks. I began to have serious doubts about the black-and-white, good guy–bad guy history I learned from high school and Hollywood.

While I was recollecting memories of World War II stateside, my wife, Shizuko, who as a baby embarrassed her mother by crying during an American air raid on Tokyo, also had some memories. She grew up amid the wreckage of a city where more people died than at Hiroshima, foraging for edible weeds. Her mother, still alive at 106 at the time of this writing, had once shopped for vegetables with Hideki Tojo's wife. Her older brother had been a kamikaze pilot and saw the family house burn. Shizuko's family did not understand the total picture any better than I did, but my dealings with them convinced me that all Japanese were not congenitally homicidal. Something had to be lurking beneath the surface to trigger an attack on a country with twice their population and twenty times their natural resources.

The other books on the subject were not much help. Samuel Eliot Morison's official history was written with such eloquence that I wondered if I was reading about the Peloponnesian War instead of the one I had heard about from my father and Hank Traber. Morison's references to "the gods of battle," "the Fates," and—so help me—"the Indian sign" did not ring true to me. Morison's Pearl Harbor was the opening gun of a German-

Japanese attempt to take over the world—period—despite the staggering amount of evidence that neither Japan nor Germany had wanted a war with the United States in 1941. Henry Salomon had been Morison's chief assistant. Morison ended his chapter on Pearl Harbor with a quotation from Sophocles, dead a mere 2,300 years when the bombs fell on the Pacific Fleet. Go figure.

Walter Lord was better, but he tended to ignore the question of motivation. Lord served in Army Intelligence in London in World War II, and—unlike Morison and most of the other mainstream historians—he was not a racist, though he was certainly a patriot. His one literary flop was a book he wrote in praise of the civil rights movement.

Gordon Prange, given the last word on the subject by the historical establishment, blandly dismissed the plausible warnings by the Yugoslav-German double agent Dusko Popov and the Korean patriot Kilsoo Haan of an attack on Pearl Harbor. The latter even had the date right. The United States certainly took these two seriously *after* the attack. Both Popov and Haan were threatened with retribution if they went public with news of their attempts to warn the government.

On the other hand, John Toland in *Infamy* mingled some very plausible information—including slightly convoluted accounts of Popov and Haan—with some outright nonsense. Toland was on the right track, but his occasional problems with accuracy undermined what could have been a strong case. He had the concept right but his facts were all over the map.

Still worse was Harry Elmer Barnes. In his account, Franklin Delano Roosevelt, who supposedly inherited a deep love of China from his grandfather, deliberately planned the attack on Pearl Harbor. FDR's grandfather, Warren Delano, was an opium trader, and his views on the Chinese, as revealed by my friend and former editor Geoffrey Ward, were contemptuous and deeply racist.

Delano once accidentally shot and killed a Chinese boatman, gave the widow $150, and told her the accident was the best thing that could have happened to her family. He despised an American who treated his Chinese concubine like an actual wife and loved his half-Chinese children. People of that ilk do not lose sleep over Japanese atrocities, real or fake, and this kind of family sentiment did not launch World War II.

The man who came closest to the truth was Herbert Romerstein, co-author of *The Venona Secrets*. A dropout from high school communism and later a U.S. counter-intelligence worker, Romerstein based his hatred of communism on what he saw as a soldier during the Korean War. The Koreans are a great source for the facts about the evils of communism, but their objectivity on Japanese foreign policy is open to question. When it rains on a Korean wedding, the Koreans wonder how the Japanese made this happen. Romerstein, with his affection for the hard-working and generally lovable Koreans, failed to see that Japan did not want a war with the United States in 1941 and did whatever it could to avoid such a war. The Koreans, however, cannot otherwise be discounted as observers. They courageously opposed Japanese and Russian colonialism as the Japanese opposed American and European colonialism. A historian needs both a Japanese and a Korean perspective if he is to understand why Japan attacked Pearl Harbor.

CHAPTER 1

MEETING OF MASTERMINDS

Vitalii Pavlov groped through his pocket and finally came up with two quarters and a dime. He was nervous. At twenty-seven, Pavlov was the second in command of Soviet espionage operations for the NKVD in the United States, following a purge in which Josef Stalin had murdered many of the senior agents. Successor to the Cheka and predecessor of the KGB, which replaced it in 1946, the NKVD was a murderous agency with its own foreign policy. Pavlov had arrived in the United States a month earlier, in April 1941, and was still fumbling through a new world of cultural confusion. Blond, handsome, self-conscious about his shaky command of English, and in over his head in the lethal world of espionage, Pavlov was on a mission of importance far beyond his years or experience.

Pavlov slid into a phone booth in Washington, D.C., and shut the door. He inserted the coins into the unfamiliar telephone, heard the clink and jangle, and dialed. The phone started to ring. He said later that he felt time had stopped. Someone picked up at the other end.

"White here," the voice said.

"Mr. White, I'm a friend of your old friend Bill," Pavlov said. "Bill is in the Far East and wants to meet with you when he comes back. He wants you to meet with me right now."

Harry Dexter White was the director of the Division of Monetary Research of the U.S. Treasury Department. "Bill" was Iskhak Abdulovich Akhmerov, a Russified Tatar NKVD agent posing as an expert on China whom White had met two years earlier on the recommendation of Joseph Katz, yet another NKVD agent and active "first line" spy recruiter. Katz was co-owner of a New York City glove manufacturing company which operated as a cover. Akhmerov, a Bolshevik since his teens in 1919, with dark hair, narrow eyes, and a square classic profile, was handsome in a Hollywood tough-guy way that women found fascinating. Katz, who wore alarmingly thick eyeglasses, full dentures, and walked with a limp, spoke German, Lithuanian, Russian, and Yiddish. He was a superb middleman in the world of espionage because he looked nothing like a spy.

"I have a pretty busy schedule," White said nervously. Pavlov was ready for this. NKVD sources had described White as a dedicated communist sympathizer and a source of information since the mid-1930s, but also as timid and rather cowardly.

"I'm only going to be in Washington for a few days, and it's important to Bill that you meet with me," Pavlov said. "If you can give me half an hour at Old Ebbitt Grill, I'll pay for the lunch."

"How will I know who you are?" White asked.

"I'll try to get to restaurant a few minutes before you do," Pavlov said, sensing agreement. "I'm of average height, blond hair, and I'll be carrying a copy of *New Yorker* and leave it on table."

"All right," White said reluctantly.

Pavlov had breakfast the next day with his handler, an NKVD agent known as Michael, and went over the details as they rode to the Old Ebbitt Grill in a Soviet embassy limousine. Michael reminded him that White was a senior official of the United States government and that Pavlov should not make any offer that included outright treason, for fear of entrapment and the notoriety that entrapment might bring. Michael reminded Pavlov that he was protected by a diplomatic courier's passport, and even if White refused to help and turned him in to the FBI, Pavlov himself would be safe—though with the tacit understanding that Comrade Stalin did not like people to fail.

Michael probably knew, even if Pavlov did not, that Rudolf Hess, Hitler's most devoted follower and the top Nazi fluent in English, had flown to a meeting with British aristocrats on May 10 to make an astounding offer. Britain, then apparently losing the war with the Hitler-Stalin alliance, could have peace with Germany if Britain agreed to stay neutral in the coming clash between Germany and Russia. Hitler offered to evacuate France, Belgium, the Netherlands, Norway, and Denmark, keeping only German-speaking Luxembourg and Alsace-Lorraine, if Winston Churchill stepped down as prime minister and Britain gave Germany a free hand in Eastern Europe. The control of Russian farmland and resources had obsessed Hitler since he and Hess hammered out *Mein Kampf* in 1923–1924. Churchill would not step down. The British did not trust Hitler, and they, like the Germans, wrote off Rudolf Hess as a self-promoting lunatic. But the NKVD knew that

Britain's consideration of Hess's proposed alliance could not be ignored. It comported with Britain's traditional hostility to Russia and its more recent fear of communism.

"Comrade Akhmerov's ideas are all compatible with the national security of the United States," Michael told Pavlov. "White is already anti-fascist, so make sure to emphasize that these ideas are dictated by the need to counteract German fascism and Japanese militarism.... Tell him that we anticipate a Hitlerite attack on our country, and, by protecting us from the aggression of Japan in the Far East, he will assist in strengthening the Soviet Union in Europe. Anything that helps bridle Japanese expansion in China, Manchuria, or Indochina would be equally useful to us and to the American interests in the Pacific region. If you need to, remember to mention the Tanaka Memorial."

The Tanaka Memorial, supposedly Japan's scheme for a world takeover, was a Soviet forgery that dated back to 1931. The Russian forgers claimed it was a memorandum from Gi'ichi Tanaka, a soldier in the Russo-Japanese War and the Japanese prime minister in 1927, just after Emperor Hirohito's ascension to the throne. The Tanaka Memorial detailed the need to conquer first China, then Russia, then Western Europe, and finally North and South America. When renegade Japanese communists translated the Tanaka Memorial from its original Russian, its expressions were so foreign to Japanese thought and idiom that it was instantly recognized as a fake.

Michael had just described to Pavlov what Soviet intelligence had code-named "Operation Snow." For the Soviet Union to be able to fend off a German attack from the west, the Japanese threat from the east would have to be neutralized. A war between Japan and the United States would achieve that goal nicely. Pavlov's job was to find a friend in the U.S. government with enough influence over American policy to subtly but effectively provoke that war.

Pavlov was calm when he arrived at the Old Ebbitt Grill to meet White and found an empty table. He set out his copy of the *New Yorker* and noticed with satisfaction that he was the only blond customer in the dining room. A few moments later, Harry Dexter White walked in. Pavlov recognized him from Akhmerov's description—energetic if slightly pudgy, with a small dark moustache and metal-frame glasses. Pavlov took him to be between thirty-five and forty years old, though White in fact was almost fifty. His childlike timidity made him look younger than he was.

Pavlov stood up. "Mr. White."

"Mr. Pavlov," White replied as he walked over. Pavlov noticed that White had mild, sad eyes. As they were shaking hands, the waiter walked up.

"May I take your order?"

"You can just order breakfast for me," Pavlov said. White spoke to the waiter and then turned back to Pavlov.

"I must apologize for my barbarous English," Pavlov said. "I've been living in China long time, far from civilization."

"I don't believe that will prevent us from getting to know one another," White said gently. (This was an ironic remark. White had tried to teach himself Russian—with little success—so he understood Pavlov's problem. In Chinese and Japanese, as in Russian, there are no definite and indefinite articles, and people who translate their thoughts literally into English tend to sound rather primitive even if the thoughts themselves are elegant or profound.)

"Bill sends you his regards," Pavlov said. "He's friend of mine, but he's actually more like an instructor, whom I deeply respect—you understand?"

White nodded with approval.

"Bill has told me little bit about you," Pavlov said. "He asked me for a favor which I willingly granted. He emphasized that I should try to be very genuine and that it was impossible to postpone the message until he returns home and can meet you."

"When is Bill coming to the USA?" White asked.

"Bill wants to come back as soon as possible, no later than end of this year," Pavlov said. "He is trying to figure out the American and Japanese attitudes. The expansion of Japan into Asia has him constantly alert. This is why he asked me to meet you, only if you didn't object, to get acquainted with the idea that he's most involved with right now."

Pavlov was lying. Akhmerov was not in China—he was in Moscow under detention. Akhmerov had broken protocol by romancing and marrying an American communist, Helen Lowry, a niece of Earl Browder, the highly visible leader of the Communist Party of the United States. Stalin's paranoid binge of executing his own followers had brought Akhmerov back to Moscow to answer charges, and he had been spared execution but put on hold. Akhmerov was eagerly awaiting the results of the dialogue between White and Pavlov.

"I had a good impression of Bill when I met him a couple of years ago," White said. "He's obviously a very wise person. I'll be glad to listen to you."

"I must apologize again for my lack of English knowledge," Pavlov said with a smile. He dipped into his breast pocket and put a small, folded note on the table in front of White, next to the *New Yorker*. White unfolded the note and read it carefully. His eyes betrayed astonishment and apprehension, but his mouth and breathing were under tight control as he read an outline of Operation Snow.

"I'm amazed at the concurrence of my own ideas with what Bill thinks, according to this," White gasped, to explain his visible response. His pudgy face was pale. White tried to tuck the note into his own breast pocket, but when Pavlov stuck his hand out for it he tamely gave it back.

"I'm going to China in couple of days, and Bill wishes to know your opinion," Pavlov said. "In fact, he is so worried whether he is going to see a management of the USA of the Japanese threat, and whether something will be done to bridle the Asian aggressor."

"You can tell Bill this from me," White said nervously. "I'm very grateful for the ideas that corresponded to my own about that specific region.... I've already started to think about what is possible and what is necessary to undertake... and I believe with the support of a well-informed expert, I can undertake necessary efforts in the necessary direction.... Did you understand everything I just said?"

"You are very grateful of ideas that correspond with your own about that specific region.... You have already started to think about what is possible and what is necessary to undertake... and you believe with the help of well-informed expert, you can undertake necessary efforts in necessary direction."

White nodded with satisfaction. "Karasho," he said in Russian with an American accent. "Your memorization is very good.... Let me pay for lunch.... I ordered it."

When Vitalii Pavlov walked out of the Old Ebbitt Grill, he was a "made man" in Soviet intelligence. He survived subsequent paranoid purges as Stalin slipped into senescence, and he later retired as a lieutenant general of the KGB. Akhmerov, the mastermind behind the plot, was restored to Stalin's good graces and was back in the United States by September, in charge of the most successful NKVD spy operation in history. Akhmerov would remain head of the Soviet espionage program in the United States until 1948. Katz fell from favor when he admitted he was not man

enough to kill Elizabeth Bentley, "The Red Spy Queen," after her
defection. Bentley had always said she found the gentle little cripple likable, so sentiment may also have been involved. Katz was
shuffled back to Europe. Harry Dexter White, a trusted assistant
to Franklin Delano Roosevelt's close friend and secretary of the
Treasury, Henry Morgenthau Jr., had just bought Vitalii Pavlov
lunch. White had also accepted a written NKVD order on behalf
of Josef Stalin to protect the Soviet Union's Pacific flank. He had
agreed to provoke a war between the United States and Japan.

CHAPTER 2

AGENT OF
INFLUENCE

Harry Dexter White was never actually a member of the Communist Party USA. He worked under deep cover, posing as a conventional, rather conservative economist whose specialty was international financial relations. On the surface, he never ventured farther to the left than his one-time hero John Maynard Keynes, the British economist. Behind the scenes, White was the brains behind Henry Morgenthau Jr., who in turn tried to be the brains behind Franklin D. Roosevelt.

Roosevelt, an Anglo-Dutch patrician from the Hudson River Valley of New York, coasted to success after Groton and Harvard through his double relationship to President Theodore Roosevelt—once remotely through birth, and again more intimately through marriage to his cousin Eleanor, TR's niece. People who had watched Franklin grow up said that the family's main problem would be preventing him from becoming president of the United States. The girls at the Seven Sisters colleges, who were courted by Ivy League men, used his initials—FDR—as an abbreviation for "feather duster" and thought of him as a light-weight, though he was a good football player and a marvel on the dance floor.

Roosevelt was never a communist. He was an astute, intuitive politician with a liberal program—which the Depression made imperative—who thought he could use the communists, just as the communists thought they could use him. FDR, in fact, had been preconditioned to dislike radical politics by two events that could have cost him his life. Two narrow escapes may have convinced him that he was a man of destiny and also that a benign authoritarian government was vital to the interests of his own family and social class.

In 1919, when he was assistant secretary of the Navy, Roosevelt was at a somewhat bibulous party with Attorney General Mitchell Palmer, who asked him for a ride home. Roosevelt, whose own drinking was under control at that point, gladly obliged. Palmer asked Roosevelt to stop off for a nightcap in his home library, but Roosevelt declined the offer. Palmer went straight to bed and Roosevelt drove away. That night, an anarchist dropped off a bomb that blew up the library and could have killed Roosevelt and Palmer if they had sat up drinking there. The anarchist himself was killed by the premature explosion of the bomb.

On February 15, 1933, Roosevelt, then the president-elect, was in Miami, Florida, to deliver a speech. Crippled by then with polio, Roosevelt was sitting atop the back seat of a convertible. Giuseppe Zangara, an Italian-born anarchist with mental health problems, popped up from the crowd and started shooting. A woman hit Zangara's arm with her purse, and his shots struck four other people, including Mayor Anton Cermak of Chicago, but not Roosevelt. Whether these random homicide attempts predisposed FDR to favor authoritarian government—communism, or, in its earlier days, Nazism—is anybody's guess, but he clearly believed that the best government was the government that protected the common man from himself.

Roosevelt relied heavily on his secretary of the Treasury, Henry Morgenthau Jr., the scion of a German-Jewish family whose large fortune was built by Henry Morgenthau Sr. The first member of the family in America, Lazarus Morgenthau, emigrated from the Kaiser's tolerant Germany, where a prosperous and overwhelmingly loyal Jewish community had enjoyed full civil rights for almost a century. Lazarus, however, was near-bankrupt in the most prosperous era in German history. He stayed near bankruptcy in America, backing inventions he could not market, such as a "tongue scraper." He was a gifted eccentric. His son, Henry Morgenthau Sr., more gifted and not at all eccentric, made a substantial fortune in New York real estate. A force in the Democratic Party and a strong supporter of Woodrow Wilson, Morgenthau was unable to obtain a cabinet-level appointment—prejudice against Jews was strong in large parts of the Democratic constituency—but he was able to win appointment as ambassador to the Ottoman Empire in 1913. He distinguished himself in that position by bringing the Armenian genocide to the attention of the West and is honored as a hero by the Armenian people. He was a brilliant man, an exemplary citizen, and a genuine humanitarian.

Henry Morgenthau Sr. and his wife had three daughters and one son, Henry Morgenthau Jr. The boy was something of a disappointment at first. His father sent him to Cornell, where he studied architecture, possibly with an idea that he could help run the Morgenthau family's massive real estate operations, but young Henry never finished college. Morgenthau eventually set Henry up as a gentleman farmer on an estate propitiously near the property of Franklin and Eleanor Roosevelt. His path to success in the Democratic Party was paved by his father's intelligence, reputation, and money. Morgenthau's government service began in the Department of Agriculture and later brought him to the Treasury. He was governed throughout his career by two concerns: a decent attempt to defend the Jewish community from its worst threat since Roman times and a constant fear of offending the Hudson Valley grandee who gave him his cabinet job despite his shaky academic and intellectual qualifications.

Harry Dexter White—his birth name was either Weit or Weiss—came up the hard way, not as a rich man's son like Franklin Roosevelt or Henry Morgenthau Jr. Born on October 29, 1892, he was the youngest of the five sons of Jacob Weit, a Jewish peddler who came to America from Lithuania when that Baltic nation was an unhappy part of the Russian empire. White later appropriated the name Dexter from an Anglo-Saxon friend. White's Jewish ancestors had been persecuted by the tsarist regime, often out of resentment for their intelligence and learning, just as he himself—small, clumsy, annoying in his intelligence—was persecuted by ruffians in the tough working-class Boston neighborhood where he grew up.

Despite this background, White had aspirations. He belonged to a grade-school reading group that met one night a week at the Webster Literary Club, where each boy would read a composition he had written. White's hard-working father eventually owned four hardware or crockery stores, and he moved his wife, Sarah, and the seven children to suburban Everett, where Harry attended high school. His grades were mediocre. After graduating, he took over his father's hardware and crockery business with two of his brothers but did not like it. In 1911, Harry was admitted conditionally to the Massachusetts Agricultural

College (today's University of Massachusetts) after failing the U.S. history and civics entrance examinations. He stayed in college only one semester, leaving with a C+ average.

White was still working in the family business when the United States declared war on Germany in April 1917. Four days after the declaration of war, he enlisted in the Army. His strong performance in a military science course at Massachusetts Agricultural College won him admission to Officer Candidates School, to be turned into what Army regulars called "a ninety-day wonder"—a freshly minted second lieutenant. In the wartime swirl he met Anne Terry, a student at Pembroke College in Providence, Rhode Island. Like White, she was a child of Jewish immigrants from the Russian empire—in her case, from the Ukraine. Unlike White, she was an excellent student, almost a prodigy. They married just before he was shipped overseas with the infantry.

Second Lieutenant White got to France with the American Expeditionary Force, but he never saw combat. For most of his Army career he worked at administrative jobs, including the management of an orphanage for the cast-off children of American doughboys and French and Belgian girls. He returned to the United States as a first lieutenant in 1919, left the Army with an honorable discharge, and moved to New York City, where he turned his sad experience at the orphanage for unwanted children into a job as the manager of a settlement house where poor immigrants came for help with their health, their English, and their grocery bills and rent. Day-to-day contact with poor people who lacked the intelligence and initiative of Jacob and Sarah Weit convinced Harry that the world was a cruel place and that an education was crucial. He enrolled at Columbia University in February 1922 and studied there for three semesters, earning much better grades than he did at Massachusetts Agricultural College. He transferred to Stanford

University in California and received his bachelor's degree "with great distinction" in 1924, winning the coveted Phi Beta Kappa key. The next year, he received a master's degree in economics from Stanford.

Marriage to Anne Terry and his academic success increased White's self-confidence, and he developed a "take-charge" personality. Once, driving through a small town in rural California with Anne by his side, White spotted a house fire. He parked the car, jumped out, and took charge of the volunteer firemen, who had never seen him before. Under his command, the firemen saved the furniture and most of the house. Harry and Anne rode off into the sunset like the hero and heroine of a cowboy movie.

White's next stop was Harvard, where he earned a doctorate in economics in 1930. He then began teaching economics there as an adjunct professor, as well as at Simmons College in Boston.

White did not obtain a permanent position at Harvard. William James had demanded that Harvard accept Jewish professors at the turn of the century, but there was still an unspoken but palpable quota. So in 1932 White moved with Anne and their two daughters to Appleton, Wisconsin, and joined the economics faculty at Lawrence College. The same year, Lionel Trilling became the first Jewish instructor in the English department at Columbia, Trilling's own alma mater and the most liberal campus in the Ivy League. "My appointment to an instructorship in Columbia College was pretty openly regarded as an experiment and for some time my career at the College was conditioned by my being Jewish," Trilling would recall. He was summarily—and unfairly—dismissed in 1936 and told that as "a Freudian, a Marxist, and a Jew" he would be "more comfortable" somewhere else. Trilling, who preferred the classics to the moderns and actually despised Stalinism, talked them out of it, and by the time he finally became a full professor in 1948, he was one of the most popular figures at Columbia and generally regarded as America's greatest living literary critic.

Students interviewed by *Time* magazine in the 1950s did not think White was anything like Lionel Trilling. They remembered him as "an excellent instructor but a distant, arrogant man who thought that the White opinion was the only opinion." His classroom teaching was standard conservative economics, but his one book, based on his Harvard dissertation, contained tributes to Lauchlin Currie, who read the manuscript, and George Silverman, who clarified certain points. Both would later be exposed as Soviet agents.

In June 1934, as Franklin Roosevelt and his advisors were struggling to lift the United States out of the Great Depression, Harry Dexter White was tapped for a summer assignment at the U.S. Treasury by Jacob Viner, an internationally known economist from the University of Chicago who was said to be an even tougher professor than White. Viner was a liberal but not a communist and part of FDR's famous "Brain Trust." White wrote some memoranda on the gold standard and international trade that attracted notice in the administration. The New Dealers were struck by the transformation of the United States from a land of self-sufficient farmers and craftsmen into an industrial power with international ties. Many of these men were simply warm-hearted Americans who felt sorry for the poor and the downtrodden. Others were closet communists or, like White, intense communist sympathizers.

White's affinity for communism went through two phases. In the first phase he was a communist in everything but name and an active conduit of U.S. government secrets. In the second phase, he dived for cover after a serious scare and posed as an ostentatiously loyal American while his betrayals grew more furtive—and more lethal. He seems to have become an admirer of Soviet communism around 1934, about the time he came to Washington. Almost immediately, he began passing classified information to agents of the Soviet Union.

Whittaker Chambers, an alcoholic poet and translator who later repented and became a celebrated informer, was an active communist courier when he met White in 1935.

"Harry Dexter White, then the chief monetary expert at the Treasury Department, had been in touch with the Communist Party for a long time, not only through his close friend, George Silverman, but through other party members whom he had banked around him in the Treasury Department," Chambers remembered years later in his book *Witness*. "He was perfectly willing to meet with me secretly; I sometimes had the impression that he enjoyed the secrecy for its own sake." Chambers noted that White preferred to meet him near White's own apartment on Connecticut Avenue. "Since White was not a party member, but a fellow traveler, I could only suggest or urge, not give orders. This distinction White understood very well, and he thoroughly enjoyed the sense of being in touch with the party, courted by it, but yielding only so much as he chose."

White passed Treasury Department information to Chambers—whom he knew only by his code name, "Carl"—usually by furtively taking the classified papers out of the building and handing them over to Chambers, who had them photographed over night. The secret papers were returned in the morning to White, who replaced them before anyone knew they were missing. Sometimes Chambers photographed the documents himself. "Carl" was protective of White's reputation. After one communist courier kept White waiting on the street for an hour, Chambers refused to work with the tardy photographer again. The man's sloppy schedule had placed White at risk. "I held that any communist who would endanger a man like Harry White by coming an hour late to an appointment was unfit for underground work." Chambers was a romantic drunkard and a would-be man of the barricades until he dropped out of the party. He never actually liked White, who was both a bully and a sycophant in his bureaucratic job. He was not a man of the barricades as far as Chambers was concerned.

"I sometimes found myself wondering why I troubled to see him," Chambers remembered. "But when once, quite by chance, I kept away from him for two or three weeks, I discovered that he was plaintive and felt himself neglected by the party, was very friendly and cooperative." White was obsessed with pleasing his boss, Henry Morgenthau Jr., and could be made depressed and worried by a single gruff remark. "Whenever the Secretary was snappish... White had one of his crises of office nerves." White's attitude toward his own subordinates, however, was described as condescending, almost brutal. He found just about everyone he had to deal with to be his intellectual inferior, and said so—as long as he did not have to work for him. Oddly enough, he also had a sense of humor when he was not threatened. When a secretary was bold enough to tell him that his little mustache made him look like Hitler, White dryly said that he had grown his own mustache first and Hitler must be imitating him.

In 1936, Whittaker Chambers was given a new handler, Boris Bykov, then the head of Soviet military intelligence in the United States, whom Chambers also disliked. Bykov, a Jewish anti-Semite who once panicked at the sight of a rabbi, spoke almost no English and committed constant behavioral blunders. Bykov struck Chambers—translator of Felix Salten's *Bambi* from German to English—as crass and ignorant, possibly dangerous. Chambers found Bykov's wife to be attractive, stupid, and scared. He said that Bykov was the only Russian he had ever met who did not like children—he would curse when they crossed his path—and Bykov's wife was the only Russian he had ever met who could not understand German, the second language of most Russians of the time. Bykov's English was so bad that he and Chambers usually conversed in German. In moments of tension, Bykov would sometimes lurch into desperate outbursts in German, even when they were conversing on the street. Chambers found this nerve-racking.

When Bykov suggested that the underground informers in the United States government be paid for their information, Chambers was aghast. Chambers felt—and he may have been right—that the Soviet agents were supplying information out of loyalty to Marxism or disdain for snobbish upper-class America, rather than out of simple greed.

"Money!… They would be outraged," Chambers said. "You don't understand. They are communists on principle. If you offer them money, they will never trust you again. They will do nothing for you."

Bykov, however, insisted, as usual lapsing into German in a moment of tension: "Siehst du, wer auszahlt ist der Meister, und wer Geld nimmt muß auch etwas geben." ("You see, he who pays out is the master, and he who takes money must give something for it.") Chambers decided that communism had begun to corrupt itself from within. His romantic views of the barricades gave way to disgust at the provincialism, moral squalor, and quirks of men like Bykov.

"You will lose every one of them," Chambers predicted.

Bykov and Chambers compromised. Chambers agreed to buy some expensive Oriental rugs made by child labor in isolated parts of Soviet Asia and bestow them on top informants. Bykov gave Chambers a thousand dollars to buy the rugs. The son of a shabby-genteel family who prided himself on his indifference to luxury, Chambers delegated the bribe-buying to a friend who knew something about rugs, Professor Henry Meyer Schapiro of Columbia— without telling Schapiro that the rugs were the wages of treason.

Harry Dexter White was one of the four informants who got a rug. His friend George Silverman was another. Chambers later saw the rug at White's house.

A decade later, another communist courier also saw the telltale carpet at White's home.

"Why, that looks like one of those Soviet rugs," the female agent said. White appeared very nervous, and the carpet had vanished by her next visit.

Bykov's blunders nearly exposed White's friendship with the Soviets, Chambers remembered. Once a black Washington carpenter named Harry White received a container of caviar from the Soviet embassy. Then he was surprised to receive a case of vodka. Next the mail brought an engraved invitation to a reception at the embassy. The astounded carpenter soon received a telephone call from Harry Dexter White, who had discovered that a black carpenter who shared two-thirds of his name was receiving expensive gifts from the Soviet embassy. White the federal bureaucrat timidly suggested that White the black carpenter keep half of the largesse and return the other half.

"I was going to send them all back to him, but I thought: he's the kind of fellow, that if I send them all back, will still think that I kept half. So I did."

The crunch came for Chambers in 1938 when he decided to drop out of the party and out of espionage. Starting in 1937, Russian-born agents were being recalled to the Soviet Union by the NKVD and in many cases charged, tortured, and shot for offenses that at least some of them never committed. The disappearance of a couple whom Whittaker Chambers knew personally, a Latvian forger known as Adolph Arnold Rubens and his American-born wife, Ruth Marie Boerger, became notorious among Soviet agents. The couple was recalled to Russia, where Arnold was executed. Ruth was resettled in Kiev and never heard from again. Chambers remembered sadly how, before leaving New York, Mrs. Rubens had worried that she would not be able to find tomato juice for her baby in Moscow. Bykov, who hated children, found this hilarious. He nicknamed her "Tomato Juice."

Even more notorious was the disappearance of Juliet Stuart Poyntz, a blue-blooded intellectual, charter member of the CPUSA, and a Soviet agent who was disillusioned by Stalin's purges. After revealing her intention to leave the party and expose Stalin as the murderer he was, Poyntz disappeared. The story hit the New York newspapers in December 1937. Whittaker Chambers knew her well and was obviously terrified that he might be next.

"What happened to Juliet Poyntz?" Chambers asked Bykov.

"Gone with the wind," Bykov shrugged and smiled.

The enormity of Stalin's purges—which struck the Red Army, the ranks of loyal Bolsheviks, and religious believers—had given a lot of the earlier romantic communists sick stomachs or cold feet. Chambers had already experienced a whole-hearted disillusionment with communism and the beginning of a religious conversion when, in 1938, he himself received a summons to Moscow for some re-education. Chambers took this to be a possible death sentence and decided to make a clean break with the party. He stole some papers from his cycle as a Soviet courier and hid them in a pumpkin patch at his farm in Maryland. Some of the "pumpkin papers" were in Harry Dexter White's own handwriting and contained information about Japanese politics and economics. Chambers's wife was to hand the papers over to the FBI if he was kidnapped. The wild forbidden romance with communism was over. Communism—the hope of the downtrodden outside the Christian fold during the worst of the Depression—stood revealed to Chambers and many other dropouts as a bloody, brutal farce.

Aware of what was going on in Russia, Chambers nervously thought about confronting White in his office at the Treasury

Department, where he was unlikely to encounter any NKVD killers sent to shut him up. He could not get past the uniformed guard at the Treasury building without giving his name, and since White knew him only as "Carl," there was no point in trying. So Chambers called White from a pay telephone in a drug store across the street from the Treasury building.

"Mr. White.... This is Carl. I'm just across the street at the drug store and I need to see you right away."

"I'll be right down."

White bustled in, obviously delighted to see Chambers again.

"Back on a little trip to inspect the posts?" White asked.

"Let's go for a walk," Chambers said. White chattered on about his all-important relationship with Secretary Morgenthau while Chambers braced himself. They sat down for coffee at a candy store.

"Are you coming back to Washington to work?" White asked.

"No, I am not coming back to Washington to work. I am not here to 'inspect the posts.' The fact is that I have broken with the Communist Party and I am here to break you away from the apparatus. If you do not break, I will denounce you."

White stared silently into his coffee, obviously terrified.

"You don't really mean that," he said.

Chambers explained that he was dead serious and that if White did not stop passing information to the Soviets he would be turned in to the FBI. White swore to quit—so sincerely that Chambers believed him. A few months later, when Chambers filed a detailed report with Adolf Berle, an anti-communist liberal and the security officer of the State Department, White was one of the two contacts Chambers did not name. Chambers believed at the time that Harry Dexter White had dropped out of the espionage network for good. Chambers probably never knew about White's role in provoking Pearl Harbor.

In August 1939, the Molotov-Ribbentrop Pact, a treaty of non-aggression between Nazi Germany and the Soviet Union, was signed in Moscow, carving up Poland between the two powers. Soviet communism was finished as a haven for most idealistic leftists. George Orwell, who had joined the Republicans in the Spanish Civil War, witnessed Stalin's betrayal of the Spanish anarchists, who actually believed in freedom and human rights, and became a lifelong and outspoken anti-communist. The purges of 1938 and the Molotov-Ribbentrop Pact moved Arthur Koestler, a Hungarian Jew who had served as a Stalinist agent in Spain and narrowly escaped a Nationalist firing squad, to write *Darkness at Noon* and turned him into a lifelong anti-communist. Budd Schulberg, whose novel *What Makes Sammy Run?* made him the *enfant terrible* of Hollywood, had joined the Communist Party in opposition to Hitler. He found the party's interference with his artistic freedom offensive and finally left at the time of the Molotov-Ribbentrop Pact. These defectors from a cause they once admired, and in some cases risked their lives for, joined the novelist Ayn Rand, the screenwriter Ben Hecht, and many others in rejecting a nightmarish ideology that had already destroyed tens of millions of lives.

Harry Dexter White, almost incredibly, was still a believing communist. Frightened by Chambers's defection and the bloody purges in Russia, he stayed inert for three years until Pavlov reactivated him under threat of a dire emergency. By May 1941 the NKVD saw that the Molotov-Ribbentrop Pact was about to collapse but that Stalin refused to believe it. Vitalii Pavlov's reactivation of a man who had been out of the loop for almost three years was sparked by a growing desperation concerning the future of the Soviet Union.

CHAPTER 3

RED STAR
VS.
RISING SUN

J apan had been a threat to eastern Russia since its startling victory in the Russo-Japanese War, and Britain and the United States had nurtured the rise of Japan as a counterweight to Russia. Stalin might have been paranoid, but by mid-1939 Japan indeed posed an existential threat to the Soviet Union.

Japan's military forces, which sometimes operated almost autonomously from the Diet in Tokyo, were polarized into two hostile factions. Strike North, dominated by the Chosu clan from Honshu, the largest Japanese island, and in control of the Imperial Army, saw Russia as Japan's natural enemy. They prepared for war on the Asian continent. Strike South, dominated by the Satsuma clan from Kyushu, the big southern island and the wellspring of

Japanese culture, controlled the Imperial Navy and saw the colonial powers of Britain, France, and the Netherlands as the enemy. They prepared for war in the Pacific. All Japanese sentimentally regarded their nation, the only real industrial power in Asia and possessor of the world's third largest Navy, as the defender of "colored" people everywhere. The Japanese, in fact, had attempted to insert a clause into the charter of the League of Nations recognizing the equality of all races but were rebuffed by the British.

Whatever their racial sentiments, Britain and the United States did not want Russia in the Pacific, and they supported Japan's development into a modern military power. In 1902, with an eye on Germany, a potential Russian ally, and its perennial rival France, Britain entered a treaty with Japan promising its assistance should the Japanese find themselves at war with more than one power. In the Russo-Japanese War of 1904–1905, Japan enjoyed diplomatic support from Britain and financial support from the Jewish-American banker Jacob Schiff. Outraged at the tsar's failure to act when dozens of Jews were brutally murdered in Russia, Schiff floated a loan that helped Japan prosecute the war to a successful conclusion. Theodore Roosevelt, an outspoken admirer of Japan, gave copies of *Bushido*, Inazo Nitobe's interpretation of the samurai code of chivalry, to his friends. Nobody told Roosevelt that Nitobe, a Christian convert married to an American woman who stuffed their house with garish Victorian furniture, had offered up a rather prettified version of *bushido*, the way of the warrior. Roosevelt knew less about the Japanese than he thought he did, but he did understand that they could be dangerous to cross—a lesson that his successor and cousin, Franklin, would learn the hard way.

Theodore Roosevelt had less regard for Korea, a country which he saw as incapable of self-government. In 1905, his secretary of war, William Howard Taft, reached an understanding with the prime minister of Japan, Taro Katsura—the so-called Taft-Katsura Agreement, described in a secret and informal memorandum that did not become public until 1924. In return for a free hand in the Philippines, America acceded to Japan's domination of Korea. The United States turned the Philippines into a plantation while Japan attempted to absorb Korea into its empire. Though the Japanese gave the Koreans their first public schools, banks, and railroads, they earned a reputation for extreme cultural arrogance and brutality, employing rape as a form of crowd control.

Russia's defeat to Japan in 1905 touched off the discontent with the tsar's government that set Russia on the road to revolution. The valor and discipline of the victorious Japanese soldiers, on the other hand, had impressed Western observers, Theodore Roosevelt among them. As he guided the belligerents to peace at Portsmouth, New Hampshire, the president sought to check the rising sun of Japanese power. The Treaty of Portsmouth, which ended the Russo-Japanese War and earned Roosevelt a Nobel Peace Prize, provoked a furious reaction in Japan. Convinced that they had been swindled, Japanese mobs burned thirteen Christian churches and every police station in Tokyo. The delegates who signed the treaty were gently told once they got home that they might want to commit suicide because of their disgrace.

In America, sentiment began to turn against the Japanese, particularly in the organized labor movement on the west coast and among the politicians who needed its support. After the San Francisco earthquake of 1906, Japanese, Chinese, and Korean children were removed from their neighborhood schools and concentrated in a single segregated school. Japanese-Americans and the Imperial Japanese government were outraged. Faced with a recalcitrant school board in San Francisco, President Roosevelt came up with the Gentlemen's Agreement between the United States and Japan. According to this informal understanding, the

U.S. would not enact restrictions on Japanese immigration (as it had done with Chinese immigration in the 1880s), and San Francisco would end its segregation of Asian students. In return, Japan would on its own halt the immigration of its nationals to the United States. The Japanese glumly swallowed the insult and turned their attention to consolidating their hold on Korea.

In 1909, the former Japanese prime minister and resident general of Korea, Hirobumi Ito, who had demanded concessions from Korea at gunpoint but stopped short of outright annexation, was assassinated by a Korean patriot gunman in Manchuria, then controlled by tsarist Russia. Japan responded by annexing Korea the following year and launching a new crackdown.

During World War I, the Japanese honored their treaty with Britain by mopping up German possessions in China. The Germans, whose Kaiser Wilhelm II invented the threat of the "Yellow Peril," admitted that they were treated decently once they surrendered, and some opened businesses in Japan. The Japanese built 123 merchant ships for Britain in shipyards safe from predatory German U-boats, and they sent their Naval forces to the Mediterranean, where a German U-boat torpedoed a Japanese corvette escorting a British convoy, killing seventy-seven Japanese sailors. The Japanese also rescued Armenian and Greek fugitives from the war that started when the Greeks and Turks redressed their postwar borders with reciprocal massacres. Perhaps more to the point, the Japanese sent troops to fight the Bolsheviks for Siberia.

On March 1, 1919, President Woodrow Wilson's "Fourteen Points" touched off a peaceful demonstration of Koreans inspired by Wilson's principle of self-determination for all nations. When Korean hoodlums on the fringe of the demonstration robbed a few shops and killed a few Japanese, the Japanese unleashed the Korean National Police—a mixed force of Japanese and Koreans—and Japanese troops, who broke up the demonstrations with gunfire, public rapes of respectable girls, and prolonged floggings of men and women alike. Sumil—March 1—became the black holiday of Korean patriots around the world and marked a watershed. Before the Sumil riots, the enormous technical and education improvements that Japan had brought to Korea made cooperation with Japan a respectable option. After Sumil, most Koreans of education and spirit became bitterly anti-Japanese. The Americans, despite protests from outraged missionaries, did nothing. The Russian threat in the Pacific—a threat that the Bolshevik revolution had intensified—kept the United States content to abide by the still-secret Taft-Katsura Agreement.

The Anglo-Japanese Alliance was up for renewal in 1922. Under pressure from the U.S. and Canada, Britain let the treaty lapse, casting its lot in the Pacific with the United States. The Washington Naval Conference, which concluded in February of that year, attempted to limit the buildup of the Japanese Naval forces. The conference limited Japan to three battleships for every five built by Britain or the United States—another insult as far as the Japanese were concerned. The Japanese compensated by building more aircraft carriers, a British innovation from World War I not yet recognized as the future replacement of the armored battleship as the most important combat vessel.

Two years after the scrapping of the Anglo-Japanese Alliance, the United States revised its immigration laws to permit exactly one hundred immigrants per year from the empire of Japan to America. Some Japanese were so outraged that they threatened to commit *hara-kiri* on the steps of the American embassy. The Smoot-Hawley Tariff followed in 1930, raising import duties to 50 percent and inflicting a terrible blow to Japan's economy.

The Japanese concocted a pretext to seize Chinese-ruled Manchuria, which was rich in raw materials. The Chinese responded with a boycott of Japanese goods and attacks on Japanese businesses. War broke out in 1932, punctuated by the brutal aerial bombing of a civilian slum in Shanghai that killed about a hundred helpless Chinese civilians. At the ensuing peace celebration, a Korean patriot named Yoon Bong-Gil threw a bomb into the Japanese reviewing stand, killing two Japanese generals. Future ambassador to the United States Kichisaburo Nomura lost an eye in the attack, and the future foreign minister Mamoru Shigemitsu lost a leg.

The first battle of Shanghai was followed five years later by a more devastating conflict, the Second Sino-Japanese War. At the start of the second battle of Shanghai, in 1937, Chiang Kai-shek's air force bombed its own city "by accident"—or to recapture the American and European sympathy aroused by the genuine Japanese bombing in 1932. American observers were startled to see how poorly the Chinese defended themselves. Those Americans who tried to assist the Chinese discovered to their dismay that the whole country seemed to operate on the basis of bribery. Chinese generals expected bribes before they would accept American donations of equipment. Chinese field commanders sometimes ran out on their men on the eve of battle. The Japanese, by contrast, fought with incredible courage and immense energy, but they also committed atrocities at Nanking and elsewhere that horrified even their most ardent admirers. The thousands of Japanese battlefield executions with bayonets and swords and the hundreds of rapes were appalling enough, even before China's friends exaggerated them far beyond reality. The departure of Chiang Kai-shek and his deputy commander, Tang Sheng-chih, before the battle of Nanking was less widely publicized.

Americans, for the most part, were more upset by the Japanese bombing and strafing of the U.S. gunboat *Panay* on the Yangtze River, which left three sailors dead and twenty seriously wounded, than they were by the Rape of Nanking. The Japanese apologized for bombing the *Panay* and sent money to the families. Japanese women chopped off their hair and sent it to the American families to show their grief. The Americans rolled over and went back to sleep. In *Too Hot to Handle*, a Hollywood movie made the next year, the war in China is treated as a joke. Clark Gable and Leo Carillo, playing news cameramen, lose footage of a mistaken Japanese strafing, so they set up a fake strafing with a kite as a Japanese biplane—just for laughs. The Chinese weren't laughing.

To the Soviets, the Rape of Nanking, with forty-two thousand Chinese dead, was insignificant compared with Stalin's purges, and the Russians had always hated Asians in any case. What worried the Soviets was a clash with the Japanese along the Khalkha River in the disputed border region between Mongolia and Manchuria. It was this incident that inspired the NKVD's frantic desire for a war between the United States and Japan.

CHAPTER 4

EASTERN THUNDER, NORTHERN FROSTBITE

Mongolia was historically of importance to both Russia and Japan. In the 1200s, the Mongols had conquered most of Russia and left a genetic and political imprint on the culture. Many Russians have Asian facial features, and arbitrary government has been a staple of Russian culture, though Russians themselves often revel in boisterous anarchy—"you can't call it a party until you've drunk the ladies' perfume."

Few Russians had ruled Russia in modern history. The Romanov dynasty, toward the end, was more German than Russian, and Lenin was the son of an Asiatic father from the Chuvash tribe and a German mother. Stalin was half Georgian and half Ossetian. His hatchet man, Lavrenti Beria, was also a Georgian, and many of his other henchmen were renegade Ukrainians or secular Jews. But it was the Mongol horde that Russians remembered. The Tatars, who lived in the Crimea, were their descendants, so feared and hated that the Russians used to call any man a "Tatar" who was merciless and brutal.

Japan had escaped a Mongol invasion in 1280, the time of the Kamikaze, or "divine wind," the typhoon that destroyed the fleet of Chinese and Korean ships bringing Mongol invaders to Kyushu. But the Mongol threat loomed large in Japanese folklore. The Japanese name for the ideographic Chinese characters used in both countries is *kanji*—"khan writing." Perhaps to forestall any future troubles, perhaps to pursue their stated policy of "Asia for the Asians," the Japanese had long-standing alliances with the various nomadic tribes of Mongolia, even after Japanese adventurers like the giant samurai Torazo Miyazaki, a friend and supporter of the Chinese revolt against the Manchu dynasty, were discouraged from playing a role in Chinese internal affairs.

By 1939, Japan and the Soviet Union were locked in a dispute over the border between Japanese-controlled Manchuria and the Mongolian People's Republic, a Soviet ally. In May, the Japanese launched a tentative incursion into Mongolia—the second in two years—near the town of Nomonhan. Scattered fighting between horse cavalry units on both sides escalated to regular infantry battles between Japanese and Russian foot soldiers.

The Japanese were surprised by the weaknesses of the Red Army. The Russian soldiers were described as "stolid" but "lacking initiative." The Japanese introduced the Russians to their unique grenade launcher, a miniature mortar or pocket cannon, later known as the "knee mortar" to U.S. soldiers in the Pacific. When their regimental 70-millimeter howitzers failed to knock out Soviet tanks, the Japanese swarmed over the older, slower Red Army tanks like ants on candy and blew them up with hand grenades or "Molotov cocktails"—wine bottles filled with gasoline and wicks made of oily rags that set the tank engines on fire and roasted the crews alive. The Russians—still numb after the NKVD purge that had wiped out half their officer corps the year before—had never seen soldiers like this and did not like what they saw. This was the so-called Nomonhan Incident, an embarrassment on the ground. It was followed by a Japanese air attack on June 27 that cost the Russians half again as many aircraft as the Japanese lost.

The Red Army struck back with its two best weapons: General Georgi Zhukov and the BT tank. Zhukov, a shrewd, tough officer who had somehow slipped through the purges two years before, reorganized around the Russians' one advantage—tanks. The Russian BT tank, the greatest in the world at that time, was designed in the United States by J. Walter Christie, the unchallenged but unappreciated genius of armored fighting vehicles. The standard Russian heavy tank, the T-35, had become an anachronism. Design features borrowed from Britain and further developed by Germans produced an underpowered 55-ton land battleship with a cramped crew of eleven men and five separate turrets, three for cannons and two for machine guns.

Christie, who designed and manufactured tractors in his factory in New Jersey, departed from conventional tank design in a way that the crusty American generals did not approve of. They preferred horse cavalry, or, in a pinch, armored cars and motorcycles. Tanks were supposed to move slowly, with the infantry, to knock out strong points when the foot soldiers could not get through the enemy machine gun fire. Christie designed a high-speed amphibious tank that could swim the Hudson River from New Jersey to New York and back again and still deflect bullets with its armor plating. Army brass and the U.S. government were not interested.

The Russians, however, were *very* interested. In 1931, they made a deal with Christie to purchase plans and two prototypes, which were shipped (illegally) to Russia, still under a trade embargo, through Amtorg, the Soviet trading company. The Christie tanks were labeled "tractors" and were shipped without their turrets and top armored decks. The Russians simplified Christie's design, adding a high-velocity 45-millimeter gun and two machine guns, and the *Betushka*—Russian slang for "Little BT"—rolled off the assembly line by the thousands. First tested in the Spanish Civil War of 1936–1939, the BT proved to be the best tank on either side.

In Mongolia, Zhukov assembled 498 BTs and other tanks and launched a counterattack in which the Japanese were battered, surrounded, and—an ominous precedent—either escaped by stealth or fought to the last man rather than give up. Both sides worked out a deal, and the Nomonhan Incident ended with about eight thousand dead Russians and nine thousand dead Japanese. The casualty rates would not have been so even without the Russians' armored attack. Before Zhukov and the BTs rode to the rescue, the Russian soldier had proved an embarrassment even in defense, supposedly a Russian specialty.

Japan had learned that suicidal valor could not compensate for feeble armored forces on the vast plains of Mongolia or Siberia. The Strike North faction, which prepared for war with Russia, found its position weakened. Russia had learned that ethnic border troops and second-string equipment could not withstand the Japanese Army. A war with Japan would be a genuine conflict and not a colonial walk-over. American statesmen of the same era did not appear to understand any of this.

Stalin understood. The Soviets did not follow up on Hitler's September 1 invasion of Poland until September 17, two days after signing the ceasefire that ended the Nomonhan Incident. The Russians knew that a two-front war on the heels of the demoralizing purges would be catastrophic.

The Germans saw that the threat to Siberia worked to their advantage. In April 1940, Duke Carl Eduard of Saxe-Coburg and Gotha was in Tokyo paying court to Japanese royals, seeking to assuage their hurt feelings over the Molotov-Ribbentrop Pact, which had paved the way for the Nazi and Soviet invasions of Poland. "There is a certain amount of mystery" surrounding the duke's visit, the *New York Times* reported on April 26. The *Times* repeated Japanese rumors that the duke had come "to mollify the twist that German foreign policy gave to the anti-Comintern axis last year." A grandson of Queen Victoria and cousin of the late tsar, Carl Eduard demonstrated to imperial Japan that Nazi Germany still admired and protected royalty, while Soviet Russia murdered them.

Russia's next mistake was based on its fear that Hitler, victor over Poland and terror of the decadent democracies, might renege on his non-aggression pact with Stalin. The Russians tried to bully Finland—once part of the tsarist Russian empire, freed with German help during World War I—into moving its border sixteen miles back from Leningrad, Russia's "window on the West" on the Gulf of Finland. When the Finns refused to shift the border, the Russians faked a Finnish attack on Russian territory and attacked Finland in "retribution" on November 30, 1939.

If the Japanese had exposed serious flaws in Red Army morale and leadership, the Finns made the Russians look ridiculous. Unprepared for Finland's intense winter cold, the Soviet troops from temperate southern Russia huddled around campfires and field kitchens and were shot by Finnish snipers who stalked them wearing white sheets as snow capes and gliding through the frozen

forests on skis. The Finns set up dummies dressed as Finnish officers in exposed positions. When Red Army snipers shot the dummies and exposed their own positions, the Finnish snipers shot
back with 20-millimeter anti-tank rifles that splattered their targets. The death-defying Finns, like the death-defying Japanese,
also knocked out Soviet tanks with Molotov cocktails—about two
thousand of them. In one battle, the Finns killed 6,000 Russian
troops and captured 43 tanks, 71 artillery pieces, 29 anti-tank
guns, 260 trucks, and 1,170 horses for a loss of 800 men. The
Russian general in charge and his two top subordinates managed
to slip past the Finns, only to be executed by their own commissars
because they had abandoned their field kitchens.

Foreign volunteers flocked to help heroic little Finland—8,700
Swedes, 1,010 Danes, 725 Norwegians, 366 Hungarians, and
several hundred Italians, British, and Americans, including the
future film star Christopher Lee. Britain and France sent aircraft,
ammunition, medicine, and food. Pope Pius XII condemned the
Russian invasion. The moribund League of Nations expelled
the Soviet Union as an aggressor. The only friend Stalin had left in
the world was Hitler. Germany attempted to block the shipment
of supplies to Finland and refused to allow idealistic German anti-
communists to serve with the Finns. Hitler's support for an attack
on Finland may have convinced Stalin—though not Soviet Army
intelligence or the NKVD—that he was a true friend and a reliable
ally. When the beleaguered Finns finally gave up 9 percent of their
pre-war territory and 20 percent of their industrial capacity in
March 1940, after a heroic fight with redoubtable military skill,
the whole world had turned against Stalin—except for Hitler and
Harry Dexter White.

CHAPTER 5

THE MAY
MEMORANDUM

Having received his marching orders from Vitalii Pavlov, Harry Dexter White sat down at his typewriter in May 1941 to change the course of history. His task was to touch off a war with Japan without being detected as a Soviet agent. He knew that the majority of the American people wanted to stay out of the war in Europe unless the United States were attacked. FDR had won huge applause, and the election of 1940, when he pledged to keep America out of the war. But White also knew that the president was concerned with saving Britain from Hitler, and that most Americans sympathized with Londoners under German air attack. The previous September, Roosevelt had sent fifty aged World War I destroyers to the British in exchange for some bases in Newfound-land and Bermuda. Then in March 1941 he had signed the Lend-Lease Act, providing loans and military equipment to Britain and provoking howls from isolationists, including men in his own party.

White himself did not sympathize with Britain. The Party line, since the Molotov-Ribbentrop Pact, was that the British had brought their troubles on themselves and that Britain and France were capitalist and colonial powers not worth saving. The Communist Party chairman, William Z. Foster, wrote, "It was not Germany who attacked France and England, but France and England who attacked Germany, assuming responsibility for the present war." Moscow, in the hope that America would stay out of the war and let Britain and France go under, opposed FDR's plans for mobilizing the United States—until the NKVD saw Hitler as a potential menace in the days just before the German invasion.

White's problem was that Roosevelt was an anglophile and not a communist, and he probably thought that a war against Japan would take manpower away from his goal of rescuing Britain. In June 1940, when the Japanese capitalized on the fall of France by moving into northern Indochina, a French colony where most people disliked the French as much as the Koreans disliked the Japanese, Roosevelt imposed an embargo on the sale of steel and scrap metal to Japan. He avoided cutting off its oil, however, a move that might have provoked war with Japan, which had almost no petroleum resources of its own. White was aware, though, that in April Roosevelt had secretly permitted pilots from the U.S. Army, Navy, and Marine Corps quietly to resign and fly U.S.-built P-40 fighter planes for Chiang Kai-shek against the Japanese. If the Japanese discovered that American mercenaries in Chinese pay were killing Japanese aviators, the war might start without White's help.

White's boss, Henry Morgenthau Jr., was outraged at Nazi Germany's persecution of the Jews, but Morgenthau was certainly no communist. He was loyal to America and to his fellow Jews but not at all loyal to Stalin. But neither FDR nor Morgenthau would have opposed a war that catered to his own concerns. Roosevelt wanted to ride off on his white horse and save England, and Morgenthau wanted to save the Jews and punish the Germans.

The real obstacle was Cordell Hull, the secretary of state. Born in a log cabin in Tennessee and said to be part Cherokee, a self-taught lawyer like Abraham Lincoln, he had served as an infantry officer in Cuba in the Spanish-American War. Hull would be tougher to persuade than Roosevelt. The author of the federal income tax laws of 1913 and 1916 and the inheritance tax law of 1916, Hull was a populist, a friend of the common man. He knew that in war it is the common man who gets killed or crippled.

Hull and Morgenthau had already had one showdown. By 1938, the persecution of Jews in much of Europe had caused a refugee crisis. Shortly after the German annexation of Austria, which left another two hundred thousand Jews stateless, Roosevelt convened a conference at Évian-les-Bains in France to try to expedite the flight of German and Austrian Jews. The problem was that while the English-speaking nations and France felt sorry for the Jews, they did not want to take them in. The British took a few, Switzerland and France took those with a lot of money, and Canada and Australia took almost none. The Dominican Republic and Mexico continued to accept large numbers of Jews. So did the Japanese Empire, but when the refugees found out that they were welcome in Shanghai and Manchuria but not in the Japanese home islands, many delayed fleeing Europe in the hope that the English and Americans would relent. Hitler found it hilarious that while everybody deplored the German mistreatment of the Jews, nobody seemed to want them.

The United States quietly accepted about twenty-seven thousand refugees a year, mostly under the quota established for Germans in 1924. The emphasis should be on the word "quietly," since nobody was supposed to mention that the refugees were (mostly) Jewish. A large part of Roosevelt's urban and southern constituencies were bluntly anti-Semitic, and he was leery of offending them. Hollywood depicted the Nazis as brutal and violent but rarely depicted their victims as Jews. (Charlie Chaplin's earnest comedy *The Great Dictator* was a notable exception.) FDR followed the Hollywood policy. The Great Depression and the Dust Bowl diverted Washington's attention from the troubling fate of Jews across the sea.

In June 1939, a year after Évian, Cordell Hull refused to allow MS *St. Louis*, a German ship loaded with 936 Jewish refugees from Nazi-occupied Europe, to dock in the United States, despite Morgenthau's urging and his assurance that "there would be nothing in the papers." Hull had bested Morgenthau, the man known as "the second secretary of state." And Morgenthau hated Hull for it. The refugees went back to Europe, and about half of them were later killed in the war or murdered in the Holocaust. Hull was not an anti-Semite by conviction. His wife was Jewish on her father's side, though she was raised as an Episcopalian. He simply wanted to avoid outraging his own constituency, conservative Americans who were sometimes anti-Semitic and, like Hull, wanted to keep out of Europe's troubles. Knowing that FDR wanted to help Britain and that Morgenthau would support a war against Germany—maybe not against Japan, where Jewish banking interests were respected and Jewish refugees were sheltered—White decided to aim a knock-out blow against Cordell Hull's quasi-isolationism.

H. D. White
May 1941
I.

The Franco-British brand of diplomacy emulated by our own State Department appears to have failed miserably. Due to half-measures, miscalculations, timidity, machinations or incompetence of the State Departments of the United States, England and France, we are being isolated and we find ourselves rapidly moving toward a war which can be won by us under present circumstances only after a costly and bitter effort and only with a terribly dangerous aftermath. Granted the necessity for being optimistic about the outcome of a war in which before many years we alone may be fighting a victorious Germany (with Japan and Italy as her allies, and with the whole of Europe turning out equipment for them), it would be fatal to let such optimism obscure the difficulty of the task confronting us and prevent us from taking drastic steps to strengthen our position while yet there remains time.

White continued for five pages, redundantly stating how important diplomacy was, and then proposed a memorandum to be sent to Japan.

II.
United States and Japan
A.

Whereas: War between the United States and Japan would cost thousands of lives, billions of dollars; would leave the vanquished country bitter and desirous of revenge; would foster social disruption, and would not insure peace during our children's lives, nor permanently solve troublesome problems now standing between the two countries, and

Whereas: The United States is eager to avoid war, and is willing to go to more than half way to settle peaceably the issues that stand in the way of more friendly intercourse between the two countries, and

Whereas: The United States recognizes that Japan, because of the special nature of its economy, is greatly in need of opportunities for increased foreign trade, and in need of capital to repair the ravages of four years of warfare, and

Whereas: The United States recognizes that injustice has been done to the Japanese people by our immigration laws, and

Whereas: The United States believes that in the long run the interests of both the Japanese people and the American people can best be served by establishing fair and peaceful conditions under which Japan and her neighbors can prosper, and

Whereas: The United States is, because of numerous circumstances, powerful enough to destroy Japan should the United States be forced against her will to take up arms against Japan, and

Whereas: The United States is rich enough in funds, raw material, equipment, and technical skill to build, if necessary, a Navy and air force ten times as strong as that which Japan can build, and

Whereas: The United States wishes so much to avoid unnecessary bloodshed and destruction that it will pay well to help Japan's economy back to a peaceful and healthy basis, and

Whereas: The United States wishes to help China maintain her independence and attain peace so that she may go forward in her political and economic development, so unfortunately interrupted in 1937, and

Whereas: The United States believes there is no basic obstacle to permanent and more friendly relations between the United States and Japan and believes that the Japanese people will welcome an opportunity to restore peace, to reconstruct Japan's industry and trade, and to promote friendly relations with her neighbors on a basis fair both to Japan's needs and the needs of her neighbors,

And finally—and of most immediate importance—

Whereas: The United States wishes to concentrate as soon as possible her Naval forces in the Atlantic so as to be prepared for any emergency against a potential enemy with whom there is no current basis for friendship.

The United States proposes to enter into an Agreement with Japan at once under which the United States and Japan will agree to do certain things, as follows:

B.

On her part, the United States Government proposes to do the following:

To withdraw the bulk of the American Naval forces from the Pacific.

To sign a 20-year non-aggression pact with Japan.

To recognize Manchuria as a part of the Japanese Empire.

To place Indo-China under the Government of a joint British, French, Japanese and American Commission, which will insure most-favored-nation treatment for those four countries until the European War is ended, and which will govern the country primarily in the interests of the Indo-Chinese people.

To give up all extra-territorial rights in China, and to obtain England's agreement to give up her extra-territorial rights in China, and cede Hong Kong back to China.

To present to Congress and push for enactment a bill to repeal the Immigration Act of 1917 which prohibits immigration into the United States of Japanese, and place the Japanese and the Chinese on the same basis as other peoples.

To negotiate a trade agreement with Japan, giving her (a) most-favored-nation treatment and (b) such concessions on imports as can be mutually satisfactorily arranged, including an agreement to keep raw silk on the free list for 20 years.

To extend a $3 billion 30-year credit at 2 per cent interest, to be drawn upon at a rate not to exceed $200 million a year except with approval of the President of the United States. Half of the funds to be used to purchase the products of the United States, and the remainder to be used to purchase commodities of Latin American countries.

To set up a $500 million stabilization fund half supplied by Japan and half by the United States, to be used for the stabilization of the dollar-yen rate.

C.

On its part, the Japanese Government proposes to do the following:

Withdraw all military, Naval, air police forces from China (boundaries as of 1931) from Indo-China and from Thailand.

Withdraw all support—military, political or economic—from any government in China other than that of the national government.

Replace the yen currency at a rate agreed upon among the Treasuries of China, Japan, England and United States all military scrip, yen and puppet notes circulating in China.

Give up all extra-territorial rights in China.

Extend to China a billion yen loan at 2 per cent to aid in reconstructing China (at a rate of 100 million yen a year.)

Lease at once to the U. S. Government for 3 years such Naval vessels and airplanes as the United States selects, up to 50 per cent of Japan's Naval and air strength. Rental to be paid to be equal to 50 per cent of the original cost price per year.

Sell to the United States up to half current output of war material—including Naval, air, ordnance and commercial ships on a cost-plus 20 per cent basis as the United States may select.

Accord the United States and China most-favored-nation treatment in the whole Japanese Empire.

Negotiate a 10-year non-aggression pact with United States, China, British Empire, Dutch Indies (and Philippines).

D.

Inasmuch as the United States cannot permit the present uncertain status between the United States and Japan to continue in view of world developments, and feels that decisive action is called for now, the United States extends the above offer of a fair and peaceful solution of the difficulties between the two countries for only 30 days. If the Japanese Government does not indicate its acceptance of the proffered agreement before the expiration of that time, it can mean only that the present Japanese Government prefers other and less peaceful ways of solving those difficulties, and is possibly awaiting the propitious moment to carry out further a plan of conquest.

In the event that Japan elected to reject the offer of peaceful solution under terms herein indicated, the United States would have to shape her own policy accordingly.

The first step in such policy would be a complete embargo on imports from Japan.

White's proposed bribe and the demand that Japan lease half its Naval and air forces to the United States, if made public, would have sparked riots in Tokyo and rebellion in Korea. He had drafted a virtual declaration of war. But he had overstepped himself. He went on in section III of the memorandum to try to split the Soviet Union from the Molotov-Ribbentrop Pact. Despite Stalin's alliance with Hitler, his participation in the dismemberment of Poland, and his infamous attack on Finland, White suggested that the United States extend a ten-year credit of $500 million to the Soviet Union, entertain up to five thousand "technical men in the United States as students or experts in our industries," and invite fifty Soviet Army and Naval attachés to participate in U.S. military maneuvers. He also urged an embargo against any country at war with Russia—Britain was the only candidate—and wanted to require that Russia place an embargo on Germany and the countries the Germans had captured a year before. Russia was then selling Germany the oil that powered the Luftwaffe's bombing of London and the U-boats that sank British and neutral ships.

One of White's stated goals was to "...reduce communist propaganda in the United States." Another was to weaken Germany. But after the whole world had condemned Russia for the destruction of Poland and the amputation of a large piece of Finland, Roosevelt and Morgenthau were in no mood to accommodate Stalin—still a nominal ally of Hitler and a non-combatant enemy of Britain. White's first attempt to start a preemptive war with Japan and save the Soviet Union from fighting on two fronts did not succeed. He had stumbled over FDR's affection for Britain and America's distrust of Russia and apathy toward China.

White's opportunity would come, however, because he was the administration's ranking expert on Japan. Whittaker Chambers's "pumpkin papers" included a great deal of information about Japanese politics and economics:

PHOTOSTAT Q-1, Obverse:

1/19/38.... U.S. Naval Captain Ingersol will remain in London until English want to communicate anything to us with respect to Japan boycott or exchange controls. He is set to act solely as an agent of communications and not discuss matters. English are not now interested in economic boycott if against Japan. Some incidents may develop which will lead them to be desirous of our cooperation. We are likely to act alone only if unusually bad "incident" occurs such as another Panay incident.

Japan according to Co. Strong, has increased greatly its storage facilities for oil. Tanks built underground with two layers of thick cement and air space between as protection against bombing.

Reported yesterday through private Jap banking connection (unknown but supposed to be important) that J. [Japan] will not declare war on China for some time at least.

PHOTOSTAT Q-2, Obverse:

We have just discovered evidence of Japan "dumping" of textiles into the U.S. and are requiring importers to put up 100% bond against imports. I expect evidence of dumping will increase.

About 1 month ago the Pres. asked Sec. M. [Morgenthau] to secretly place as many obstacles in the path of imports from Japan as possible under existing regulations. We have made only little progress to date on the matter. Our purchase from Japan are declining (*illegible word crossed out*) steadily mostly on most items other than silk. Our imports average about two-thirds of last year's average. Part of the decline is due, of course, to our reduction in purchases from all countries.

Japan's dollar balances in the U.S. are not declining much. They are about 10 million dollars.

...If Japan repeats another incident like the Panay incident Treasury machinery is all ready to embargo Japanese imports into U.S. & freeze her dollar balances. This was done at the Pres. wishes. It remains unknown outside the Treasury.

Vitalii Pavlov had obviously been well informed about the future usefulness of Harry Dexter White, a man who had already supplied the Soviet Union with more information about Japan than about any other country, at least based on the surviving "pumpkin papers." He had shown no fondness for Japan as the most progressive nation in Asia and no sympathy with Japanese hostility to Russian or Soviet expansion into Asia. White saved Sundays for his wife and daughters and even taught young Jewish men about their traditions on Saturday, but he drank little, partied less, and read a great deal, besides conferring with State Department officials—some of them communists or fellow travelers and others patriotic Democrats or Republicans who did not know White himself was a Soviet agent of influence. He certainly knew about Japan's China policy as stated by Koki Hirota, the former prime minister and foreign minister:

> Since Bolshevik forces coming from Outer Mongolia and elsewhere constitute a common menace to Japan, Manchukuo and China, China must cooperate in establishing such facilities as desired by Japan as a means of eliminating that menace in areas bordering Outer Mongolia.

White, even before Pavlov reactivated him, had shown every willingness to interfere with Japan's foreign policy—which was not then anti-American but anti-Russian, as the thousands of dead Russians and Japanese of the Nomonhan Incident demonstrated. The NKVD did not pick his name out of a hat. The NKVD had read the "pumpkin papers," and not just the pages Whittaker Chambers looted from White's desk as life insurance. White was an obvious target for re-recruitment once the NKVD decided to take covert hostile action against Japan.

CHAPTER 6

WAR PLAN ORANGE

America's contingency plan for the rise of Japan as a modern military power was War Plan Orange. First conceived as early as 1897, after Japan humbled Manchu China in the first war for Korea, War Plan Orange was substantially revised in 1919, after Japan had helped evict the Germans from the Pacific and had gained control of the Mariana Islands, later to become famous as Saipan and Tinian. The plan was updated on a regular basis to reflect the size of the U.S. and Japanese fleets. War Plan Orange was a factor at the Washington Naval Conference, where the United States and Britain joined hands in 1921–1922 to preserve the Open Door Policy of free trade with China and to limit the size of the Japanese Navy.

War Plan Orange predicted that war in the Pacific would be triggered by a Japanese attack on United States territory in response to American interference with Japan's global ambition. The United States would be unable to protect its territories in the western Pacific, and Japan would be unable to effect a landing on the west coast of the United States. Since Japan had about one-half of America's population and one-tenth of America's industrial might, the outcome was obvious: the United States would push Japan back through a war of attrition, with both sides inflicting and taking losses, until the Japanese and the Americans met in a single great Naval battle near Japan. The Japanese would lose.

At any given time, about a hundred U.S. Naval officers possessed copies of War Plan Orange, sometimes referred to as "Estimate of the Situation Blue-Orange." ("Blue" was the United States and "Orange" was Japan.) The secretary of war and the secretary of the Navy received, and presumably read and signed, copies of War Plan Orange upon taking office. Most senior Naval officers were familiar with the plan.

One of the Naval officers who worked on War Plan Orange was Admiral James O. Richardson. Having worked on many of its revisions through the 1930s, Richardson found that by 1939 the plan, while valuable as a strategic concept, had become outdated in several respects. He noted the large increase in the number of Japanese aircraft carriers. Pioneered by the British near the end of World War I for stubby little biplanes, carriers were still few in number in 1919 and at the time of the Washington Naval Conference. But aircraft carriers were vital by 1939.

A Japanese counterpart to War Plan Orange was set out in *The Three-Power Alliance and the United States–Japanese War*, published in Japan in late 1940 and said to have been written by a

Naval officer named Matsuo Kinoaki, a member of the ultra-nationalist Black Dragon Society. Kinoaki predicted an American attack on Japan, followed by a fight for national survival against an arrogant and racist enemy and overwhelming odds. Kilsoo Haan, a Korean anti-Japanese operative living in the United States, claimed to have stolen a copy of the book from Kinoaki himself. Little, Brown and Co. published Haan's English translation in 1942 under the title *How Japan Plans to Win*. Japanese sources suggest that the book was actually written by a Japanese propagandist to reassure the public that Japan would have a chance for a negotiated peace if forced into war with the United States. Kilsoo Haan passed off this morale-building propaganda as inside information.

Whatever its provenance, *The Three-Power Alliance* clearly reflects basic Japanese strategy. The book says openly that any attempt to invade the continental United States or Alaska would be strategically absurd. Kinoaki recognized, because of the experience at Nomonhan, that the Japanese would be inferior to the United States in tanks and trucks. Despite the poor impression Anglo-Saxon soldiers had made on the Japanese during the Boxer Rebellion of 1900, Kinoaki had learned from World War I to have considerable respect for the American infantryman.

> The soldiers of the American Army do not seem to be weaklings. Remembering the way the American Army fought at the time of the First World War, we cannot say that they are very good at fighting, but there is something astonishing in their excellent fighting spirit. Everybody dashed at the German positions like wild boars without even thinking of their lives. Therefore England

and France were shocked to see the great number of killed and wounded American soldiers.

It is very hard to believe that the soldiers of America, the civilized country of machinery, could be so brave in hand-to-hand fighting, but we can say, from this example, that they have an excellent offensive spirit.

Of course, America being an industrial country, she sets great store by all sorts of machinery. Therefore a corps such as the armored-machinery corps [armored cars and half-tracks] is much more abundant than in Germany and is undoubtedly the best in the world. We wonder if their tank corps isn't the best too....

I would say that no matter how many hundreds or thousands or millions of soldiers the United States Army may have, we should not feel intimidated by it for the time being. It will be a menace to Japan only when the control of the oceans is seized by America. Thus it can be said that the Navy of America is what we should fear most.

Kinoaki saw the Japanese Navy as having a qualitative advantage over the United States, especially in terms of torpedo attack, speed of reloading, calmness under fire, and morale. His strategic goal—if the United States pressured Japan into an unwelcome war—was to seize Hawaii and the Philippines and force the Americans to negotiate to get them back with a minimum loss of life. He saw no hope at all of conquering any part of the North American continent.

"There is not even a single target of attack in the vicinity of the United States, whereas in the vicinity of Japan are numerous points which will naturally become targets of attack," Kinoaki said, referring to Hawaii, the Philippines, and Guam.

In the vicinity of the United States, Japan does not possess any territory of her own even as large as a cat's face. Nor does she have any battleships of her own stationed there. On the contrary, the United States is in possession of territories such as the Philippines and Guam, which are near Japan's eyes and nose....

If the war clouds between the United States and Japan become intense, the United States will make up her mind to remove her Atlantic Fleet and combine it with her Pacific Fleet.

From Japan's standpoint this fact is of the utmost significance. As a matter of fact, many military experts are of the opinion that Japan will act at least before the combination of the United States Atlantic Fleet and the United States Pacific Fleet.

If Japan acts at this period, it may be said that she has chosen the best time.

We do not think, however, that military action, no matter how quick Japan's action may be, can be carried out before the combination of the two fleets. But I certainly think that the time for Japanese action will come when the United States Fleet departs for Pearl Harbor after its combination, or when it is finally on the point of carrying out a positive action after its successful arrival in Hawaii.

In the former case, Japan will not be directly menaced, but in the latter case Japan will feel a great menace.

Suppose that Japan, with generosity and farsightedness as her principle, clings hopefully to her diplomatic conversations with the United States and confines her action to scouting the movements of the United States Fleets

concentrated in Hawaii—if these United States Fleets
depart westward from Pearl Harbor, Japan cannot lose
even a second; she should launch a Naval attack like a
lightning flash.

Bluntly put, get them before they get us. This was the operating
principle of both sides in the impending showdown in the Pacific.

While the ink was still drying on the first edition of *The Three-
Power Alliance* and before Kinoaki's treatise showed up in Tokyo
bookstores, Roosevelt turned the strategist into a seer by ordering
the newly designated Pacific Fleet to Pearl Harbor.

Admiral Richardson, commander in chief of the United States
Pacific Fleet, knew War Plan Orange backward and forward but
obviously had not seen the Japanese counterplan. From the outset,
Richardson did not understand the reason for what he was ordered
to do or what he was supposed to accomplish. But he understood,
both intuitively and intellectually, that sending the major portion
of the U.S. fleet, minus the detached Atlantic Squadron, to Hawaii,
starting on April 2, 1940, would be seen as a threatening move in
Japan.

The original orders called for the fleet to remain in Hawaiian
waters until May 9, 1940, as a brief training operation and then
return to San Diego and the other bases on the west coast. But
Richardson received a dispatch from the chief of Naval operations,
Admiral Harold Stark, on April 29, 1940, telling him not to take
the fleet out of Hawaiian waters because Italy might enter the war
against England and France. Richardson was understandably
puzzled and sent a letter to Stark on May 1, voicing his "firm conviction that we urgently need a re-estimate of the situation of the
United States in world affairs and a reconsideration of our basic
war plans based on such an estimate. I strongly believe that such

a re-estimate and reconsideration will result in a firm determination to remain out of the present conflict in Europe and Asia.

"I hope that nothing will delay the arrival of the Fleet at its normal bases on the Pacific coast."

On May 4, 1940, Richardson received a dispatch from Stark, who as a young Naval officer during Theodore Roosevelt's presidency had sailed with the Great White Fleet on its round-the-world voyage to intimidate Japan: "IT LOOKS PROBABLE BUT NOT FINAL THAT THE FLEET WILL REMAIN IN HAWAIIAN WATERS FOR SHORT TIME AFTER MAY 9TH·WILL EXPECT TO APPRISE YOU FURTHER MONDAY OR TUESDAY NEXT" (i.e., May 6 or May 7).

On May 7, Stark sent another dispatch to Richardson:

CINCUS [Richardson] MAKE IMMEDIATE PRESS RELEASE IN SUBSTANCE AS FOLLOWS: I HAVE REQUESTED PERMISSION TO REMAIN IN HAWAIIAN WATERS TO ACCOMPLISH SOME THINGS I WANTED TO DO WHILE HERE X THE DEPARTMENT HAS APPROVED THIS REQUEST

PARAGRAPH—DELAY FLEET DEPARTURE HAWAIIAN AREA FOR ABOUT TWO WEEKS PRIOR TO END OF WHICH TIME YOU WILL BE FURTHER ADVISED REGARDING FUTURE MOVEMENTS X CARRY OUT REGULARLY SCHEDULED OVERHAULS OF INDIVDUAL UNITS, MOVEMENTS OF BASEFORCE UNITS AT YOUR DISCRETION. 7 MAY 1940

James Otto Richardson was an honest man. Deeply spiritual, he sometimes saw life's ups and downs as providential. He did what he could to make sure that the black cooks and mess boys on the Navy's ships had the same chow and bunks as the white sailors. He also sent his officers around to gather up the anti-British communist propaganda literature that was sometimes left scattered around when civilians visited the ships on patriotic holidays during the two-year honeymoon of the Molotov-Ribbentrop Pact. Richardson was troubled at being asked to report that he had asked for the fleet to remain in Hawaiian waters when in fact he had wanted to leave as quickly as possible.

"This was the second time the [Naval] Department had put the Commander-in-Chief of the United States Fleet in a completely false position, with a requirement that he announce to the public something which, on its very face, every tyro ensign would recognize as a phony," he said many years afterward in *On the Treadmill to Pearl Harbor*. "I did not resent being told to do something by orders from above, but I did resent being told how to do it, particularly when that 'how' made a perfect 'nitwit' out of me."

Through the following weeks, Richardson continued to receive orders to stay in Hawaii. He was ordered to release some of his pilots for training at Pensacola, orders he resented, since pilots trained in carrier landings would be needed to fly top cover over the fleet in case of trouble. Good pilots were especially important since the fleet's F4F Wildcat and second-string Brewster F2A Buffalo fighter planes were notoriously tricky to land because of their pigeon-toed retractable landing gear. Green pilots often damaged the stubby Wildcats and Buffalos in carrier landings. Richardson continued to bombard Washington with reasons for the Pacific Fleet to operate from San Diego and the other west coast seaports. Naval paint and solvent and dry dock facilities were inadequate at Pearl Harbor. The fleet was short of the 5-inch, 38-caliber ammunition used in the main batteries of destroyers and in the secondary and long-range antiaircraft batteries of battleships, cruisers, and aircraft carriers. "The Fleet was in no condition to move West of Hawaii [against Japan] because of this critical shortage."

On May 22, Richardson wrote to Stark bluntly asking to be told, once and for all, what he and the fleet were doing in the Hawaiian Islands while Hitler was overrunning Europe and Japan showed no signs of hostility.

> (a) Are we here primarily to influence the actions of other nations by our presence, and if so, what effect would the carrying out of normal training (insofar as we can under the limitations on anchorages, air fields, facilities and services) have on this purpose? The effect of the emergency docking program and the consequent absence of task forces during the training period must also be considered.

> (b) Are we here as a stepping off place for belligerent activity? If so, we should devote all our time and energies to preparing for war. This could more effectively and expeditiously be accomplished by an immediate return to the West Coast, with "freezing" of personnel, filling up complements, docking and all the rest of it. We could return here upon completion.

Stark finally sent Richardson a reply that was "one of the most direct replies to any of my letters to him, although it was far from being as definite as I would have liked."

Why are you in the Hawaiian Area?

Answer: You are there because of the deterrent effect which it is thought your presence may have on the Japs going into the East Indies. In previous letters I have hooked this up with the Italians going into the war [against Britain and France, not the United States]. The connection is that with Italy in, it is thought that the Japs might feel just that much freer to take independent action. We believe that both the Germans and the Italians have told the Japs that so far as they are concerned she, Japan, has a free hand in the Dutch East Indies.

Stark told Richardson, who had recently worked as his top assistant, that he himself did not know how long Richardson was supposed to remain in Hawaii, but that he was trying to find out. He also said he was "moving Heaven and Earth to get our figure boosted to 170,000 enlisted men (or even possibly 172,300) and 34,000 Marines. If we get these authorized I believe you will be comfortable as regards numbers of men for the coming years."

A month later, on June 22—the day France acknowledged defeat and signed an armistice with Hitler that was actually an alliance—Stark wrote to Richardson, "Tentatively decision has been made for the fleet to remain . . . where it is. This decision may be changed at any time."

Stark and Richardson were able to work out an arrangement so that married sailors and petty officers could leave for the west coast with returning ships to spend some time with their families, but the bulk of the Pacific Fleet remained in Hawaii. Richardson later said that, in his personal opinion, Stark had agreed with him that the fleet could better be prepared for an eventual war at San Diego and the other west coast bases, but that Stark had quietly been told by FDR that the fleet was staying in Hawaii. Richardson continued to send memos to Stark and to the secretary of the

Navy, Frank Knox, giving reasons why the fleet would be better off on the west coast: lack of sea-going target sleds for large-bore gunnery practice, lack of ranges for machine gun practice, and, perhaps most important, the difficulty of persuading men to re-enlist when they were based so far from their families. Richardson noted that a high enlistment rate was important and that the re-enlistment rate had fallen from 80.81 percent to 75.45 percent during Fiscal Year 1940, and to 71.49 percent during Fiscal Year 1941. Enlisted men, one of Richardson's subordinates told him, did not desire duty in the Hawaiian Islands. The married men were too far from their families and the single men said the soldiers got all the girls.

Richardson did not know it at the time, but Joseph C. Grew, the United States ambassador to Japan, was quietly notifying Washington that the Japanese foreign minister had said to him "that the continued stay of our fleet in those waters constitutes an implied suspicion of the intentions of Japan vis-à-vis the Netherlands East Indies and the South Seas.... [T]he emphasis which the Minister placed upon this matter is an indication of the important effect on Japanese consciousness of the stay of our Naval forces in Hawaii."

Yosuke Matsuoka replaced Koki Hirota as Japan's foreign minister in July 1940, after Hirota had provoked the wrath of the Army commanders by trying to negotiate an end to the war with China. After his samurai family's fortune was lost, Matsuoka was sent at age thirteen to the United States to join his older brother as a manual laborer. He lived in Portland, Oregon, with William Dunbar and his sister, Isabelle Dunbar Beveridge, who treated him like a son. Matsuoka helped support himself and the Dunbar family by selling coffee door to door, wiping tables in a restaurant, and translating for Japanese labor contractors. He was becoming American—samurai don't wipe tables. He eventually entered the University of Oregon and received a law degree in 1900.

Under the influence of the Dunbars, Matsuoka converted to Christianity. Despite the political drawbacks in Japan, Matsuoka clung tenaciously to the faith without ever sacrificing his absolute political allegiance to Japan. "While I am a Christian, I am a Matsuoka Christian. I don't believe in a lot of the things they have attached to the regular sects of America and Europe."

Matsuoka believed that it was his mission and filial duty to keep the peace between Japan and the United States. When Mrs. Beveridge died, Matsuoka, by then a veteran of Japanese politics and chief executive of the South Manchurian Railway, paid for her impressive marble tombstone out of his own pocket, the ultimate Japanese act of filial piety and obligation. Though he was a Methodist rather than a Catholic, in international affairs Matsuoka's views mirrored those of the pope—the villain was Russian-style communism.

Matsuoka was so favorably disposed to America, in fact, that as the Pacific Fleet lingered in Hawaii, Admiral Kichisaburo Nomura was sent to Washington as ambassador to counterbalance the pro-U.S. leanings of the foreign minister. Nomura, a Japanese giant at six feet tall who had lost an eye in the Korean bomb attack at Shanghai in 1932, had met Franklin Roosevelt when the future president was assistant secretary of the Navy during World War I and had been unimpressed by his intelligence. But Nomura liked Americans in general, and he appreciated the vast industrial power of the nation. Like Matsuoka, Nomura wanted peace with the United States. These two figures, one avidly pro-American, the other temperately so, had to contend with the very development—the deployment of the Pacific Fleet to Hawaii—that Japanese war planners had long foreseen as the catalyst for a Pacific war.

On July 2, Admiral Richardson had lunch with Clarence Gauss, U.S. consul-general in Shanghai, and Admiral Claude

Bloch, Richardson's predecessor as commander of the fleet and a specialist in Naval intelligence. Gauss had just come from Washington and told Richardson and Bloch that, in his opinion, "FDR and Hornbeck are handling the Far East policy and the disposition of the Fleet."

"Hornbeck" was Stanley K. Hornbeck, the State Department's indestructible expert on Far Eastern Affairs. Born in Massachusetts of old English, Dutch, and German stock who had lived in America since colonial times, Hornbeck was the son of a Methodist minister with health problems, who took his wife and Stanley, his only son, to Colorado while Stanley was still a child. Young Hornbeck graduated from the University of Denver, taught high school Latin for a year, and then became Colorado's first Rhodes Scholar. After a year at Oxford, Hornbeck went to the University of Wisconsin, where he earned his doctorate in political science. In 1909 he landed a teaching position at Chekiang Provincial College in Hangchow, China, an attractive and cultured city that was still in the throes of warlord resistance to the Chinese Republic. While in Hangchow, Hornbeck witnessed an incident that he did not understand. The warlords told the people of the city that they had weapons with magic bullets that could go through walls, turn corners, and seek out victims like bees or bats. Or so Hornbeck was told—he never actually learned how to speak more than a few polite phrases of Chinese. The populace panicked, a quarter of the population fled Hangchow, and all the others cringed in their houses. When some student desperadoes broke into the arsenal, they found four antiquated Gatling guns dating from the U.S. Indian wars fifty years before, with one magazine each, and some old muskets and trident spears. Hornbeck drew a simple message from this—"Orientals" were cowardly and easily intimidated by threats and technology.

He would believe this stereotype of Asian cowardice for the rest of his life. His Chinese-American biographer, Shizhang Hu, who generally admired Hornbeck, pointed out that he had missed the sequel to the "magic bullets" of Hangchow. After the panic subsided, the student militants discovered that modern weapons actually *had* been concealed in the arsenal, and the caretaker and his son were executed.

Hornbeck returned to Wisconsin in 1913, convinced that he was an expert on China. He favored the Open Door Policy of John Hay. China should not be colonized by foreign powers, official spheres of exclusive European or Japanese influence should not be recognized, but Americans should not be subject to Chinese courts of law or police until China was completely stabilized—the policies, in short, that the United States had always practiced in China and had practiced in Japan until the Japanese defeated Russia and evicted Germany from Asia. Much as Hornbeck claimed to love China, Chinese scholars then and now have always considered him condescending and racist.

Hornbeck's *bête noire*, however, was Japan. As early as 1916, when Japan was a useful ally of Britain, he considered it a threat. When America entered World War I, Hornbeck became an advisor on Far Eastern affairs to President Woodrow Wilson. He attended the Paris Peace Conference and the Washington Naval Conference. After lecturing at Harvard, Hornbeck joined the U.S. State Department as the chief of the Far Eastern division, responsible for both China and Japan. The Japanese seemed to trip over Hornbeck every time they turned around, and they despised him.

Hornbeck survived the drastic shift from the Republican hegemony of the Coolidge and Hoover years and was named one of four special advisors to Secretary of State Hull. Although he became the Roosevelt administration's leading expert on China and Japan,

Hornbeck was not universally admired. Joseph C. Grew, the ambassador to Japan, called the pro-Chinese Hornbeck "the epitome of that all embracing American conscience" that made Grew's own job difficult. Assistant Secretary of State Breckinridge Long regarded Hornbeck as unreasonably anti-Japanese with "a rather violent mentality" and "a rather dangerous man where delicate matters are concerned in which he has a violent prejudice." One of Hornbeck's own subordinates said that he was "irascible and pigheaded. He antagonized people in any meeting." Clark Howell, FDR's personal friend and the editor of the *Atlanta Constitution*, described Hornbeck as "... intensely pro-Chinese and anti-Japanese. He lived and taught school in China and his attitude is largely controlled by his former affiliations there." Henry Morgenthau Jr., on the other hand, thought Hornbeck was "so anti-Chinese and pro-Japanese" that some people questioned Morgenthau's grasp of reality. No one else—not even in China—thought Hornbeck was a friend of Japan.

Hornbeck was not a warmonger. He was a believing Christian, a confirmed anti-communist, and a man of conscience. He sincerely believed that intimidating the Japanese with economic sanctions, and above all, with American Naval power, could keep them in their place and allow the United States to maintain a status quo in which America would protect China militarily and quietly dominate the huge Chinese market economically. He opposed committing American troops to any clash between China and Japan; the threat of force, he believed, would make the use of troops unnecessary. Admiral Richardson, also a religious man of conscience, may have shared some of Hornbeck's convictions but was unimpressed by his brand of diplomacy.

"If I am a small man, and after an unfriendly argument my big-man opponent takes a threatening position in regard to me,

I may be restrained thereafter in what I say or do," Richardson said of the situation in mid-1940.

> If, however, the man with whom I have had my unfriendly argument is smaller than I am and known to be less capable than I in the manly art of fisticuffs, then his moving in close may well be welcomed by me as an opportunity to settle the matter by a quick punch to my jaw.... [T]hat part of the United States Fleet in the Pacific, in its state of unpreparedness and in a peace posture, was the small man vis-à-vis the Japanese Fleet. This was true because the Japanese Fleet was superior to the Pacific contingent of the U.S. Fleet in all categories, except possibly battleships, and was in a war posture as a result of its continuing war with China.

In late September 1940, when the fleet had been in Hawaii for five months, the world got an object lesson in failed intimidation of Japan. Earlier that month, the Japanese had asked Vichy France, an anti-communist state allied with Hitler, to stop allowing the Anglo-Americans to ship war materiel to China. When the Vichy French temporized, the Japanese invaded Tonkin, the northernmost part of French Indochina, to cut off American supply routes to China via the Haiphong-Yunnan Railway. The Japanese at this point controlled China's entire seacoast and the only other access to China was the Burma Road between China and British-controlled India. The French Foreign Legion put up a *baroud d'honneur*—Arabic and French for a "brawl of honor." When the Japanese landed a dozen tanks and forty-five hundred troops near Haiphong, the Vichy government asked Japan for an armistice, and the railroad was effectively closed. The battle for Tonkin ended on September 26, 1940. The next day, Japan signed an alliance with

Germany and Italy—the Tripartite Pact—but made no overt move against the British, Dutch, or American possessions in the Pacific. Matsuoka, who still hoped for peace with the United States, also concluded a non-aggression pact with the Soviet Union, which was still allied with Germany. With Italy, Russia, France, and now Japan bound by pacts and treaties to Hitler, and with Czechoslovakia, Poland, the Netherlands, and Belgium occupied by German troops, the British Empire was the only industrial democracy in the world still at war with the Third Reich.

The United States responded to Japan's incursion into a European colony—even one allied with Hitler—with an embargo on the sale of American steel and scrap iron. The Japanese, however, were more worried about their supply of oil, and they began to negotiate with the Dutch East Indies government in Batavia to increase its commitment of oil to Japan in case of further embargoes by the United States.

The scrap iron and steel embargo made the situation in the Pacific even more difficult, and Admiral Richardson made the second of his two trips from Hawaii to Washington in October 1940. On his previous visit, Richardson had told Roosevelt that the fleet was not ready for war. In October, Richardson spoke plainly—or as he put it later, "The discussion waxed hot and heavy." Richardson said that the president seemed more concerned with winning the November election than he did with preparing the fleet for a possible war with Japan. Finally, when it became apparent that Roosevelt had no intention of accepting his recommendations for an increase in the strength of the fleet, Richardson put it bluntly: "Mr. President, I feel that I must tell you that the senior officers of the Navy do not have the trust and confidence in the civilian leadership of this country that is essential for the successful prosecution of a war in the Pacific."

"Jim, you just don't understand that this is an election year and there are certain things that can't be done, no matter what, until the election is over and won."

While Hitler was bombing London and U-boats were sinking British ships in the Atlantic, Franklin Roosevelt was running for an unprecedented third term as president of the United States—and 80 percent of Americans polled said they wanted to stay out of war unless the United States were attacked. The Selective Training and Service Act, the first peacetime conscription in American history, was passed in September over the protests of pacifists and conservatives alike. The first twelve-month draft notices went out in October. Roosevelt desperately wanted to help Britain, but he also desperately wanted to get reelected. He defused some of the anger aroused by the draft in a speech in Boston on October 30: "And while I am talking to you mothers and fathers, I give you one more assurance. Your boys are not going to be sent into any foreign wars. They are going into training to form a force so strong that, by its very existence, it will keep the threat of war far away from our shores." Two days later he reassured voters in Brooklyn, "I am fighting to keep our people out of foreign wars. And I will keep fighting." And the following day in Buffalo, "Your president says this country is not going to war!"

FDR was reelected handily. The fleet that was not going to war, however, stayed in Hawaii instead of returning to the Pacific coast as Admiral Richardson constantly requested.

The next shock came from Great Britain, locked in a war with Germany and Italy and—at least by proxy—with the Soviet Union, which provided Germany with oil and wheat while the Luftwaffe was bombing London and sinking merchant ships in the Atlantic. The British had begun to refine their airborne torpedo tactics in secret even before the war in Europe began. On the night of

November 11–12, 1940, in an operation plagued by constant accidents but saved by great courage and skill, twenty-four two-man Swordfish biplanes of the Royal Navy were launched to attack the Italian fleet anchored at Taranto on the Apulian coast with a mixture of flares, dive bombing, and aerial torpedoes. Three of the Swordfish did not make the target because of mechanical problems, and two were shot down. Two aviators were killed and two were captured. The Italian Navy lost half its strength in one night. Three battleships were damaged so badly they required months of extensive repair to be made seaworthy. One battleship was taken out of the war permanently. A cruiser was also hit by bombs that failed to detonate and that would have caused another sinking if they had. This was the first air-only attack on capital ships, and it stunned the world.

Richardson reacted responsibly. Before Taranto, the Pacific Fleet had spent most of its time in Hawaii anchored in the open sea off Lahaina, on the island of Maui. Alerted to the danger of torpedo attack, Richardson moved the fleet to Pearl Harbor, where the shallow waters made aerial torpedo attacks, as he understood them, impossible. Torpedoes "could not be used against berthed ships. Our then operating air torpedoes dove very deep when launched, and took some hundreds of yards before rising to their desired running depths. They did not arm until about back at running depth." Pearl Harbor was only thirty-five to forty feet deep, and the torpedoes with which Richardson was familiar would crash into the bottom of the harbor and be rendered useless. In vulnerable situations, anchored ships were sometimes screened by torpedo nets, heavy-duty mesh that dangled underwater from floats to detonate or entangle torpedoes launched from destroyers or submarines. Richardson did not think torpedo nets were called for at Pearl Harbor. As he wrote to Admiral Stark on November 28, 1940, "I think torpedo nets within the Harbor are neither necessary nor practicable. The area is too restricted and ships, at present, are not moored within torpedo range of the entrances."

Other matters had to be considered. The miserable performance of the Italian ship-borne antiaircraft guns at Taranto showed that the offense—torpedo and bomber aircraft—now had the edge over the defense—antiaircraft guns on ships. The Army had multiple batteries of 3-inch antiaircraft guns and 50-caliber Browning machine guns stationed around Pearl Harbor. Army airfields with P-40 and obsolescent P-36 fighter aircraft could also compensate for the weak antiaircraft power of the fleet. While the Navy had 50-caliber machine guns aboard ship, it lacked the 20-millimeter Oerlikon cannons that it wanted for the short-range batteries. The Navy's medium-range antiaircraft gun, the 1.1 quadruple automatic cannon, was a stopgap measure, widely disliked by the sailors because of frequent fire stoppages and widely distrusted by the officers because the 28-millimeter (1.1-inch) slug was not heavy enough to knock down a fast-moving monoplane with a single hit, and the explosive charge was not big enough to do much damage. The Navy wanted the 40-millimeter Bofors gun, a super-heavy double- or quadruple-mounted machine gun. Chrysler had just signed a contract to produce the Swedish-patented Bofors guns from pirated British drawings, and a few single guns had been installed on destroyers and submarines, but none were available in Hawaii. The long-range antiaircraft ammunition for the 5-inch 38-caliber deck guns was still in short supply. The ships also needed basic maintenance and had to wait endlessly to get into dry dock for the scraping of barnacles and marine growth.

Richardson also wanted to establish air bases and marine garrisons on small outlying islands to provide a ring of airborne reconnaissance around the Hawaiian Islands themselves in case of trouble. He had already established long-range patrols by PBY Catalina seaplanes from the Hawaiian Islands.

Early in January 1941, Richardson took a break from his struggle to bring the fleet up to date to welcome Ambassador Nomura to Hawaii on his way to Washington. The two men knew one another casually, and Richardson cheerfully provided a U.S. Navy destroyer to escort Nomura's Japanese merchant ship into Pearl Harbor so that they could have lunch together.

"I express the professional gratitude which we feel in having a Japanese Naval Officer appointed to such a high diplomatic post," Richardson said at the luncheon for American and Japanese officers.

"The first time I had come to the United States I had come as a young midshipman just learning the rudiments of being a professional Naval officer," Nomura responded, exuding his bearish charm with a little traditional self-deprecation. "I have been back to the United States several more times, and each time I became more qualified than before. But this return finds me again a midshipman, in the diplomatic profession, just learning the rudiments of my profession." The two veteran admirals, both six-footers—Nomura was sixty, Richardson sixty-two—each looked back with satisfaction on four decades of peaceful if not always harmonious relations between their countries, punctuated by a victorious alliance with Britain, France, and Italy against Germany in World War I. Neither looked forward to a war between the United States and Japan.

Then on January 31, 1941, Admiral Richardson was informed, to his surprise, that he had suddenly been relieved as commander of the Pacific Fleet. "My orders had been a real shock to me," he wrote years later after waiting in vain for an explanation of why he had been terminated when he had been led to expect a two-year tour of duty. "I was deeply disappointed in my detachment, yet there was some feeling of prospective relief, for I had never liked to work with people whom I could not trust, and I did not trust Franklin D. Roosevelt."

CHAPTER 7

KILLING OFF THE CABINET

Crown Prince Hirohito assumed the powers of regent for his disabled father in late 1921 and almost immediately faced a series of dramatic crises. Japan in the 1920s and '30s was frequently convulsed by political turmoil of such violence that Hirohito was lucky to be alive by the time his empire went to war with the United States. The idea that the emperor enjoyed the absolute obedience of subjects who worshipped him as a god was the product of American wartime propaganda.

Hirohito's father was Yoshihito, known after his death as the Taisho emperor, the son of Mutsuhito, the Meiji emperor. Yoshihito, a tolerant and likable man, emulated European fashions—his favorite outfit was a tight-fitting German-style hussar's uniform that showed off his trim physique—and was an epic drunkard. He died of a stroke at the age of forty-six on December 25, 1926.

Hirohito's first challenge was the Great Kanto earthquake on September 1, 1923, which devastated Tokyo and Yokohama. The earthquake killed about 91,000 people, left 35,000 missing and 104,000 injured, and leveled 680,000 houses. Compounding the natural disaster, the Japanese slum dwellers turned on the Korean immigrants who had come to Tokyo looking for work in Asia's most progressive society. Amid rumors that Koreans were setting fires and poisoning wells, urban mobs murdered thousands of men whom they identified as Korean with a crude linguistic test. Those who pronounced certain shibboleths with a Korean accent paid with their lives.

Some frightened citizens tried to escape the flames by crowding into the palace grounds and were halted by the police. Seeing his moment, a Japanese communist named Sakae Osugi stood before the terrified, confused crowd and shouted: "Remember Russia, and never lay down your arms!" As the Japanese fugitives moaned and prayed, the wind turned the flames away from them and they were spared. Some of them credited the proximity of the palace. Most Japanese still feared and hated Russia after the hundred thousand dead of the Russo-Japanese War of 1904–1905, and the police soon had a full description of Osugi.

Hirohito proclaimed martial law and showed up in uniform in the crumbling ruins of Tokyo. The magnitude of the catastrophe, however, triggered responses even beyond the ethnic attacks in the slums. Coming as it did on the heels of the collapse of the Anglo-Japanese Alliance, the earthquake was taken by some—ultra-conservatives and communists alike—as an opportunity to stir up opposition to the young prince regent with his thick glasses and odd, shuffling gait. Communists began to tell Japan's disgruntled working people, often fresh from their tiny farms and driven into

the turmoil of an industrial society, that the whole capitalist imperial system was bankrupt and outmoded.

The police, however, tracked down the communist agitator
Osugi and arrested him. A police captain slipped into his cell and
silently strangled him and then strangled Osugi's wife and eight-
year-old nephew in a nearby cell. There was little sympathy for
Osugi himself, but the murder of the child outraged Japanese
women in particular, and hundreds of protests were filed by mail
and demonstration. The police captain got three years in prison
for the triple murder.

On December 27, 1923, a communist named Daisuke Namba
shot at Hirohito as he rode in a horse-drawn carriage to address
the Diet. A chamberlain riding with him was hit by shattered
glass, but Hirohito himself was untouched. The attack worried
the whole Diet—especially since the would-be assassin was the
son of a delegate. Some Diet members urged the need for economic reform, while others insisted that even the suggestion of
reform be suppressed.

At his trial, Namba bluntly asked the judge if he really believed
that Hirohito was of divine origin, and the judge declined to
answer. "I've proved the joy of living for the truth," Namba told
the embarrassed judge. "Go ahead and hang me! Banzai for the
working people and the Communist Party of Japan! Banzai for
Russian socialism and the Soviet Republic! Banzai for the Communist International!" Namba was executed two days later and
buried in a secret grave so that Japanese communists—a substantial party in the 1920s—could not turn his final resting place into
a political shrine. His disgraced father shut himself up in his room
and starved himself to death.

One Japanese biographer later noted that there had been thirty-
five public acts of disrespect toward Hirohito during his regency
from 1921 to 1926. Hirohito, unlike his father and his grandfather,

was scholarly, abstemious, monogamous, physically challenged —and unpopular with a large section of the population of Japan.

After he became emperor at the end of 1926, Hirohito attempted to win popular support. A Korean dissident, Pak Yol, and his Japanese wife, Fumiko Kaneko, had been sentenced to death for plotting to assassinate Hirohito while he was still crown prince. A photograph was circulated showing the loyal Fumiko sitting on her husband's lap while they both waited to be interrogated— which is to say tortured—at police headquarters. Hirohito commuted their sentences to life in prison, which kept them from becoming martyrs and may not have made them happy.

This act of clemency did little for Hirohito's popularity in Korea, still restive under Japanese administration despite some notable material progress. Many Koreans liked the female Japanese teachers who came to their Japanese-built schools to foster literacy and modern education and a gentle feminism at the same time. The Koreans respected the skills of Japanese physicians and engineers, and some Koreans received scholarships to study medicine and engineering. A country which had gotten by with exactly one public school when the Japanese oppressors arrived was now starting to rival Japan itself as the most education-obsessed country in the world. But the memory of Japanese brutality in the Meiji and Taisho periods filled the Koreans with a bitter hatred of the Japanese Army and the imperial family.

The dangerous persistence of this hatred became clear on January 8, 1932, when the Korean patriot Lee Bong-chang lobbed a hand grenade at Hirohito while he passed in a carriage through the Sakuradamon district of Tokyo. The grenade exploded under the wrong carriage, and the emperor was unhurt. Lee was apprehended on the spot and hanged in prison nine months later. Hirohito and the Japanese passed the Sakuradamon incident off with a joke about clumsy Koreans.

A more lethal force in Japanese politics also emerged in 1932— not the Japanese communists or the Korean patriots but dissident Japanese usually described in the West as "militarists" or "rightists." The carnage these dissidents inflicted was a shocking reality, but the "rightist" label, conjured up to equate the dissidents with European fascists, is misleading.

In the days when the Japanese and the Koreans alike were threatened by technologically superior Europeans, Japanese samurai like Hirobumi Ito and the giant swordsman Torazo Miyazaki had urged Asians to join hands and resist Western oppression while learning Western technology. Miyazaki, a Christian convert who later lapsed into drinking and womanizing but never actually recanted, was a supporter of Sun Yat-sen, the Chinese leader who spent his life trying to overthrow the corrupt Manchu dynasty and revitalize China. Sun, a Christian and a physician, dreamed of an American-style republic that would encourage Christianity and technology without rejecting the traditional Chinese virtues. Sun and Miyazaki also tried to smuggle guns to the Philippines to help the Filipinos resist American repression, which at the turn of the century was far bloodier than anything yet seen in Japanese-occupied Korea.

These were days of bold, romantic, heroic dreams, and many Japanese too young to remember them looked back with vicarious nostalgia on the days when Japan had led the rest of Asia in the struggle against colonialism and racism. The rapid industrial development that made a small number of Japanese bankers and manufacturers extremely rich had left the peasants and the new class of factory workers no better off than before. When the Wall Street crash and the Smoot-Hawley Tariff sent Japan into economic depression, many younger Japanese stopped emulating the Americans, who had undermined the Anglo-Japanese Alliance, restricted Japan's Naval power, and insulted them with restrictive immigration quotas. These Japanese "rightists" had no use for Nazi Germany, a society far more racist than the United States. Their vision was an Asia for the Asians, primarily anti-Russian and only then anti-French, anti-Dutch, anti-British, and last of all anti-American. These militants took their name from the Amur River, the boundary between Europeans and Asians that they wanted to guard. The Chinese characters for the Amur are "black dragon," and the Asia-for-the-Asians faction became known in Japanese as *Kokuryu-kai*—the Black Dragon Society.

The first important victim of Black Dragon nationalism was Prime Minister Osachi Hamaguchi, who had accepted the Washington Naval Conference's limitations on Japanese sea power, imperiling, as the Black Dragons saw it, Japan's ability to defend itself. Hamaguchi had noticed a young man stalking him but, like most Japanese born in the Meiji era, out of pride had declined to have him arrested. The stalker, a Japanese gangster named Tomeo Sagoya, caught up with the prime minister at a Tokyo railroad station on November 14, 1930, and shot him. Hamaguchi succumbed to his wounds nine months later. Sagoya was sentenced to death but never executed. He made a good living as an after-dinner speaker at nationalist banquets for the rest of his life.

By 1932, America's Smoot-Hawley Tariff had taken a ruinous toll on Japan. The nation's exports in the 1920s and early 1930s were mostly silk and porcelain. If the Great Depression alone was not enough to destroy the American market for such luxury goods, the Smoot-Hawley Tariff certainly finished it off. Japanese farmers whose sons could not ship off to California or Hawaii to find work were forced to sell their daughters as housemaids, factory workers, agricultural serfs, or even prostitutes. Bankers, who seemed to do well no matter what happened, became the stock villains for the junior officers and sergeants who saw themselves as the defenders of the common people from the exploiters who were, in their turn, dupes of the Americans and Europeans.

In 1932, a Black Dragon offshoot known as *Ketsumeidan Jiken,* the League of Blood, drew up a list of twenty prominent Japanese whom they felt must die to save Japan from the communists and the colonialists. The instigator was Shiro Inoue, a former vagabond and spy in Manchu China and later a Buddhist priest. Inoue saw capitalists, bankers, and anyone who bowed to the racist whites as the enemies of Japan. He doled out Browning automatic pistols to his followers, though only two of them carried out their missions.

On February 9, a former honor student named Tadashi Konuma, fifth son of a fisherman, killed the former finance minister Junnosuke Inoue (no relation to the League of Blood leader) as he was about to make a political speech at an elementary school in Tokyo. Inoue had been implicated in a financial scandal involving British and American banking interests before he resigned from the cabinet. His assassin was treated with great leniency by the arresting officers.

On March 5, Goro Hisanuma, a gangster, waited outside the Mitsui Bank for Takuma Dan, the leader of Japan's international banking community and a graduate of the Massachusetts Institute of Technology. "Baron" Dan, who spoke fluent English and was a friend of the Fords, the Du Ponts, and the Rockefellers, was an advocate of friendship between Japan and the United States. The night before he was killed, Dan had held a party at the Industrial Club with his American friends in international banking and asked for their help in coping with the financial crisis inflicted on Japan by the Smoot-Hawley Tariff and the world-wide depression. Hisanuma terminated Dan's illustrious career in international finance. He stepped up to Dan's limousine at the curb and shot him in the head.

Two months later, on May 15, nine military and Naval officers in their twenties paused at the Yasukuni Shrine to Japan's war dead and then converged on the private apartments of Prime Minister Tsuyoshi Inukai. The officers asked for directions, but the people they encountered sensed something was wrong and would not tell them which apartment was the prime minister's. When three or four strangers appeared, the officers shot at them. A plainclothes policeman fell, seriously wounded. The other strangers fled. Then the young officers heard a key being turned and paused to watch. Prime Minister Inukai, a trim man of seventy-five, emerged with his daughter-in-law holding his grandchild in her arms and good-naturedly invited the officers into his apartment. He was wearing a cotton men's kimono and told the young men to take off their shoes when they walked into the house.

"Now let's talk," Inukai said as he lit a cigarette.

One of the officers pulled a pistol and pointed it at Inukai's head. He pulled the trigger. The pistol clicked but did not fire. With stoic calm, Inukai adopted a fatherly manner with the tense young officers and told them that he could explain everything if they took the time to listen to him. Some of them bowed, out of an ingrained respect for an older man, and seemed ready to talk things over. "No use talking!" said Lieutenant Masatoshi Yamagishi. "Fire!" They shot the prime minister in the neck and in the face. On their way to give themselves up, the conspirators shot another policeman, threw a hand grenade at police headquarters, and threw another grenade at the Bank of Japan. Then they surrendered to the police.

Shiro Inoue gave himself up and stood trial with Inukai's assassins. The Japanese public, while generally deploring the murder, sympathized with the rage of the young officers and shared their sympathy for the peasants. The court received 111,000 signatures on a petition for clemency, and nine young peasant men each lopped off a finger, pickled them in sake, and sent them to the judges to demonstrate their own sympathy. None of the officers was sentenced to death, and while Inoue was sentenced to life in prison, he was released under an amnesty in 1940. Most of the officers were out of prison within two years, and some of the youngest were simply released with credit for the time they spent in custody during the trial.

In July 1933, forty-four members of two obscure and short-lived Japanese groups, the Love Country Labor Society and the Japan Production Society, were arrested and charged with planning to stage an uprising and wipe out the bankers, the industrialists, and those members of Hirohito's cabinet and diplomatic corps who had shown indifference to the poor and deference to the West. All were acquitted because their motives were "patriotic." Plans to put Hirohito's more affable younger brother Chichibu on the throne in his place were revealed only a decade later but were known to the secret police at the time.

Hirohito was slow to understand his unpopularity with a great many Japanese working people and his own junior officers. He was once shown a heartbreaking set of statistics. In 1932, 12,108 farm girls from northern Honshu had been sold to Tokyo labor contractors by families who could no longer feed them or find husbands for them. In 1933, that figure had climbed to over 58,000. Two thousand of the prettiest and smartest of those girls became *maiko*, apprentice geisha who might hope to better themselves as rich men's mistresses; 4,500 became common prostitutes, hapless girls who spent most of their spare time weeping and contemplating suicide; 6,000 became bar maids who tried to act like the American girls they saw in Hollywood movies; the rest became casual laborers, factory workers, or nursemaids for families who still had money.

"The farmers should not talk on and on about the unpleasant aspects of their life but should concentrate on the enjoyment of nature around them," Hirohito blandly replied.

The emperor was clearly a man of limited perspective. Members of the old nobility were not in awe of the "divine" role of emperor manufactured by the Meiji politician Hirobumi Ito in the late nineteenth century as an antidote to European colonialism and Japanese feudal warfare. Until 1935, Hirohito failed to father a male heir, a personal crisis for the first monogamous emperor in Japanese history. Some Japanese may have seen it as a curse, or at least a supernatural omen. More educated Japanese simply thought the dynasty was inbred, and perhaps an anachronism.

The country's caste system and its disruption may also explain why the Japanese, who had adapted better than any country in Asia to Western industry and technology, were nevertheless so averse to social change. Old Japan had been dominated not so much by the emperor—who existed as a sort of intercessory priest of the sun goddess—as by the *shogun*, a general and prime minister, supported by about three hundred *daimyo*, "great names," corresponding to European counts or barons, who were in turn supported by about thirty thousand *samurai*, "those who serve," trained warriors who were militarily and sexually aggressive but who protected their virtue by not handling money. Samurai were paid with rice rather than coins to prevent contamination by contact with cash.

Below the samurai was the peasant class. The Japanese peasants were not "lower class" in the Western sense but respected as central to Japan's social structure. Peasants and fishermen—slightly lower than farmers but still not degraded—produced the country's food. Peasants often served as pikemen in Japan's feudal armies or musketeers in the days before the Japanese banned the matchlock musket as socially disruptive. Those who showed real courage and keen intelligence might be adopted by the samurai and allowed to intermarry with samurai families. The young officers of the 1930s, whether of peasant or samurai ancestry—there were plenty of both—saw the two classes as bound by chivalry, sometimes by blood. To abuse the peasants was to insult the proud and fearless samurai—or more dangerous still, the upwardly mobile peasants who wanted to walk and talk and act like samurai.

Just below the peasants, and considerably below the samurai, were the artisans who produced everything from pottery to paintings. A samurai who dropped to the artisan class "lost caste" and was regarded as one who is dead—unless he was a sword maker, and thus exempt from demotion. The sword was so venerated in feudal Japan that sword makers were elevated above the artisans who made commercial goods.

The merchants were the lowest of the legitimate social classes. They were often money-lenders, never a good way to be popular in any culture. Some of them preyed on the headstrong samurai, who were not accustomed to handling money at all, or on nobles unable to meet the expenses of court appearances. Country people whispered that the merchants were secretly Chinese by ancestry, and money-lenders are the perennial villains of Japanese theatricals. The expense of elegance became staggering as the country closed itself off in the 1630s, and actual warfare all but disappeared. The importance of the daimyo nobles, who were war chiefs, and of the samurai warriors faded as that of the merchants grew during Japan's self-enforced isolation. Resentment between the classes increased with the shift from a sword-and-rice economy to a cash-and-credit economy. Industrialization and then the Depression were emotionally catastrophic for the hereditary samurai and for the peasants who had become officers and gentlemen under Japan's military system.

The lowest social class, just below the merchants, were the *eta*, untouchables whose ancestors had been butchers, tanners, and executioners in a Buddhist society where people were fond of animals and despised spilling blood except in battle. The eta class also included strolling entertainers and acrobats and common prostitutes. These hapless people were so despised that most Japanese barely acknowledged their existence. The closeness of the merchant caste to the eta—far below the peasants, much less the samurai—explains why the hotheaded young officers took such umbrage at the increasing importance of bankers and businessmen in Japanese society. No such distinction existed in America, where the Pilgrims, the Puritans, and the early Dutch settlers were usually descended from merchant families who fell back on farming and fishing because of the richness of the land and sea. The Renaissance idea of the "merchant prince" had not reached the Japanese countryside. To the Japanese peasants, money-lenders were not the Medici. They were Shylock or Scrooge.

The idealistic junior officers who saw protecting the peasants as their duty were in a seething rage over the widening gap between rich and poor. These young men admired work programs that Hitler had implemented in an over-industrialized Germany, where idled factory workers joined military-style units that marched with shovels instead of Mausers as they drained swamps and built the Autobahn. The muscular young Germans were fed and housed at government expense while they saved money and took out lottery tickets for the right to buy the first available Volkswagen, the "people's car." In the two-year honeymoon between Hitler's rise to power and the imposition of the Nazis' anti-Semitic laws and military conscription, Franklin Roosevelt himself had admired Hitler's program for a workmen's Army and copied it.

Japan's imperial government, by contrast, did little to lighten the burden on the farmers and the working poor. Some mountain peasants who lost their family farms and sold their daughters to the money-lenders climbed farther up the mountains and lived in caves, where they wove baskets and caught fish, often with their bare hands, to sell to people down in the valley. The young Japanese officers, while idealistic and perhaps naïve, were not stupid, and they were not insulated from what was happening both in Germany and the United States. They were avid readers and movie-goers, and newsreels showed them how Hitler's Germany was mobilizing to deal with the Depression, which the Japanese believed was made in the USA. The young officers despised German and American racial arrogance, but they sentimentalized Germany as the land of great music—Beethoven, Franz Schubert, and Johann Strauss Jr. were probably Japan's favorite composers of the 1930s—and they idealized America as a land where people could marry for love rather than family obligation, where the scenic wonders were impressive beyond belief, and where Walt Disney had magically shown them the world as it ought to be. The Japanese doted on Shirley Temple and Mickey Mouse. The heirs of the samurai began to plot a takeover that would reform the Army and eliminate the power of the bankers and manufacturers.

The first bloodless "Showa Restoration" plot by angry young officers was exposed in 1935, and the potential leaders were quietly placed under arrest and warned to behave themselves. Though the details of the plot are uncertain, it seems that Hirohito had again been destined for replacement by his brother

Prince Chichibu or perhaps by his infant son, Akihito, with some suitable statesman as regent for the imperial baby.

The League of Blood conspirators, two years earlier, had been inspired by a mystical Buddhism. The conspirators of 1935 were angered by the same abuse of the poor, but many of them were also inspired by the Japanese folk Christianity that had gone underground after the suppression of Catholicism in the 1630s. The *namban* villages, where Christianity survived, were the ones with no brothels or money-lenders. Statues of the Virgin Mary were disguised as Kannon, a Sino-Japanese goddess of mercy, until the distinction was lost on some people. The Japanese of the nineteenth century knew that wherever foreign missionaries went, foreign soldiers often followed, and many of them were deeply suspicious of the Western churches—though many Japanese women and some men who had studied in the United States privately remained life-long Christians and went through the mandatory state Shinto ceremonies by rote, the way Americans recite the Pledge of Allegiance. Japanese intellectuals came back into contact with Christianity by reading Count Leo Tolstoy, a figure made vastly appealing by his conversion late in life, which turned the arrogant Russian nobleman into a friend of the poor and downtrodden.

A home-grown inspiration was Kiuchi Sogo, a Japanese folk Christian martyr who made a forbidden appeal to the shogun in 1653 on behalf of the half-starved peasants in his district, who were reeling under heavy taxes they could not pay because of a bad harvest. The shogun granted the hungry peasants his mercy, but had Sogo and his four young sons crucified for daring to appeal to him in person. Sogo—called Sakura, perhaps because, like the sakura cherry blossom, he fell in his prime and not in old age—became a hero to his peasant neighbors and his house became a shrine.

The young officers' contemporary hero was Ikki Kita, a folk Christian and friend of China and the United States, who called for limits on personal and corporate wealth. Kita scorned Great Britain for its imperialism and racial snobbery, though his arch-villain was Russia, a bastion of tyranny before and after the Bolshevik Revolution.

Lieutenant Colonel Saburo Aizawa was not a Christian. He was a Shinto of fanatic intensity who believed that the hilts of his many historic swords were inhabited by the spirits of their previous owners. A fencing instructor, he knew that swords were made to be used fearlessly on Japan's enemies, foreign or domestic. In the summer of 1935, he received a posting for Formosa, then a tranquil part of the Japanese empire where many inhabitants actually liked the Japanese. The expatriate Scottish journalist Hugh Byas, who had lived in Japan for thirty years, spoke fluent Japanese, and often spent nights drinking sake or scotch with members of the Black Dragon Society, said that Aizawa had a reputation for great swordsmanship but also for mental instability. Aizawa may have seen his posting to Formosa as a step in the wrong direction if there were to be a final showdown with Russia. He may simply have been crazy. On August 12, Aizawa walked into the office of General Tetsu-zan Nagata, a confidant of the emperor. Nagata was conferring with an officer from the secret police about threats on his life when Aizawa drew his sword. The police officer blocked the first blow and was cut on the shoulder. Aizawa's hand was cut by his own sword. Nagata ran for the door, and as he seized it, Aizawa split his uniform coat down the back with a blood-splattering downward stroke, then rammed the sword through Nagata's body back to front. The general died almost instantly. As Aizawa was being led to the infirmary to have his wounded hand dressed, he walked past Nagata's body laid out on a stretcher.

"I then remembered that I had failed to kill Nagata with a single stroke, and as a fencing instructor I felt deeply ashamed," Aizawa said at his trial.

The young officers of the Black Dragon Society saw themselves as the heirs of the samurai. They intended to take Japan back from the bankers and diplomats and return to the Asia-for-the-Asians policy of Hirobumi Ito and the other legendary heroes of the Meiji era—the people who had stopped colonialism in its tracks and prevented Japan from becoming another opiated Manchu China or a death zone like American-colonized Luzon or the Belgian Congo. As Aizawa went to trial, the young officers despaired of convincing Hirohito's cabinet to alleviate the economic plight of the peasants or to recognize Russia as Japan's deadliest enemy, so they took matters into their own hands. They struck on February 26, 1936, a date that would reverberate through Japanese history as "2/26" and would have repercussions for the rest of the world as well, especially the United States.

The night of February 25 was full of festivity at the American embassy in Tokyo. Joseph C. Grew, the American ambassador, was hosting a party. A contemporary of Franklin Roosevelt at Groton and Harvard, Grew was a distant cousin of J. P. Morgan. A Republican, world traveler, college athlete, and big game hunter—he was once almost killed by a tiger in China—Ambassador Grew had been sent to Japan by Herbert Hoover after a long and successful tour of duty in Turkey. His wife, the former Alice de Vermandois Perry, was a granddaughter of the American commodore who had opened Japan to the West, and had grown up in Tokyo with many Japanese friends. Grew was sympathetic to the Japanese and committed to avoiding war between the United States and Japan.

Grew and his wife had found an unfailing enticement for their parties: first-run American movies. Dinner at the embassy that night featured good food and good liquor for the Japanese men and was followed by a screening of *Naughty Marietta*, starring Nelson Eddy and Jeanette MacDonald as a pair of sweethearts who, against all odds, marry for love. No Japanese woman could resist such a story. The men, who had enjoyed the free-flowing liquor, were comatose if not appreciative. Reality would intrude at daybreak.

At 2 a.m., the soldiers of the Tokyo garrison were awakened and harangued by their officers and sergeants about how it was their duty to save Japan by drastic action. Many of the privates were recently enlisted, and 1,359 of them joined 91 sergeants, 19 lieutenants, and 2 captains in an attempt to take over Tokyo. The other soldiers—8,500 of them and more than 100 officers— skipped the whole mission and diplomatically pretended to be asleep. The soldiers from the first and third regiments were joined by the Imperial Guards, disciplined soldiers of some standing who did not realize they were being recruited for a revolution. Snow was falling, and by 4:30 the peasant conscripts and the guardsmen had taken over a large quadrant of down- town Tokyo.

As the Japanese cabinet was sleeping off the embassy party, the junior officers struck.

At 5:05 a.m., a death squad arrived at the home of Finance Minister Korekiyo Takahashi. They shot the guard outside and caught the eighty-one-year-old minister in bed. The young officers pulled down the covers, shot him three times, and then stabbed him twice with samurai swords. He died instantly.

A former prime minister, Admiral Makoto Saito, newly appointed lord privy seal, was also surprised in his sleep. His wife tried to block the death squad but they pushed their way into his bedroom and shot him twice. His wife then desperately tried to protect him by clinging to his body as he lay sprawled on the floor. The young officers stuck their guns against his sides as he lay on the floor with his wife on top of him and pumped forty-five more bullets into him. His loyal wife was wounded but lived.

Another death squad arrived at the home of Admiral Kantaro Suzuki, sixty-eight, the grand chamberlain of Japan. Suzuki, cornered in bed with his wife, tried to explain to the young officers that their *Weltanschauung* was hopelessly naïve. He fascinated his assassins for fifteen minutes as he explained why the admirable plans of the young idealists would never work. Young Captain Teruzo Ando listened respectfully, then shot the grand chamberlain three times, keeping to the appointed timetable.

"I can still feel a pulse," the assassin told Suzuki's wife. "I shall dispatch him finally with my sword."

"If you feel that necessary, let me do it," his wife said. Ando left for a popular restaurant, and Suzuki's wife called the hospital instead of dispatching her husband. He was off the critical list in four days and lived to become prime minister in the last chaotic days of World War II.

The primary quarry of the young officers was Japan's latest prime minister, Keisuke Okada. Apparently feeling no need to appease American opinion at Ambassador Grew's party, Okada had spent the night with his mistress, a famous geisha, rather than with his wife. His housemaids shoved him into the toilet room and told him to lock the door from the inside. When the death squad arrived, the prime minister's brother-in-law, Colonel Denzo Matsuo, who looked something like him, emerged and shouted "Tenno heika banzai!"—"May the emperor live ten thousand years!" His patriotic slogan was greeted with a burst of applause from a submachine gun. He was killed instantly, and his face was such a mess that the assassins, prompted by the loyal housemaids, believed that they had killed the prime minister.

At 5:40 a.m. a group of young officers arrived at a country villa to settle up with the former lord privy seal Nobuaki Makino, one of the emperor's closest advisors. Makino escaped from the villa and ran for the trees atop a grassy hillside. The story circulated that his granddaughter had run up the hill after him to give him a final embrace, obstructing the aim of the would-be assassin, who would not fire on the little girl in her kimono. Some years later, Makino's daughter-in-law reported that the real hero was the retired police officer who shot it out with the assassins, killed one of them, and wounded a couple of others before falling himself.

Hirohito awoke on the morning of February 26 to find that fourteen hundred rebel soldiers had taken over central Tokyo with no real opposition and that his most trusted advisors were being stalked and murdered by the men who had sworn to protect him. Shoot-outs between rebel officers and retired policemen were erupting all over Tokyo and the vicinity. The emperor was dumbfounded. The rebels, led by two captains, a score of lieutenants, and fewer than a hundred sergeants commanding a gaggle of peasants, now controlled the Diet, the War Ministry, the Naval Ministry, and Police Headquarters, a short distance from the walls of the imperial palace. Hirohito moved a cot into his office, where he would be safe, and awaited developments while the rebels issued a proclamation:

> Despite the critical period ahead of us, gangs of effeminate sadists spring up in our midst like toadstools: we indulge our selfish desires and interests… we obstruct the creative evolution of all the people, causing them to groan in anguish and misery. Increasingly Japan is pursued by foreign troubles, and riding at the mercy of the waves, becomes the butt of foreign ridicule. The elder statesmen, the leaders of the Army factions, the bureaucrats, the

political parties, and so on, have all contributed as leaders
to this destruction of the national essence.... Traitorous
scholars, traitorous Communists, treasonable religious
groups are all woven together in a dark plot.... Russia,
China, England, and the United States are within a hair's
breadth, at the present outbreak, of ensnaring our land of
the gods and of destroying our culture, our bequest from
the ancestors.

To translate from their adolescent hyperbole, the young officers and
sergeants of 2/26 were asking Hirohito to respond to the Great
Depression, the Smoot-Hawley Tariff, and the depredations of the
Japanese bankers and industrialists on the samurai, peasant, and
artisan classes, the backbone of the nation and the people whom
the officers had sworn to protect. Japan's primary enemy, in their
view, was Stalinist Russia. Among their demands was the reappoint-
ment as war minister of General Sadao Araki, staunchly anti-
Russian and as committed as the young officers themselves to peace
with China and the United States.

  While the emperor and the survivors of his cabinet were digest-
ing this manifesto, it was learned that the prime minister was alive
and hiding in his toilet. The police arranged a rescue. A group of
retired police officers posed as politicians and demanded that the
young rebels hand over the body for a proper funeral. They tucked
the prime minister's heroic dead brother-in-law into an expensive
coffin. As they bore the coffin away, one of them feigned a heart
attack and fell to the pavement. The officers and soldiers on guard
rushed to watch, and the prime minister, tipped off by one of the
reliable housemaids, ducked out the back door, only to bump onto
one of the peasant soldiers, who had studied his photograph before
the raid. "Oh... it's a ghost!" the soldier gasped. Okada made it
out the back door alive, but he was finished in Japanese politics.

Hirohito stonewalled. He knew the rebels were right but did not know what to do about their complaints, so he simply refused to deal with them. The rest of the Army and the Navy, despite their anger at the money men in his cabinet, had not risen to join the rebels. Neither had they risen to defend the emperor. The government mustered 23,491 soldiers to deal with the mutineers, which the rebels had become after failing to provoke a general uprising. But nobody wanted to attack them. The mutineers controlled downtown Tokyo for three days, but they soon dispersed, defeated not by the Army but by their anxiety over confronting parental authority. Bombers dropped leaflets telling the enlisted men that they would be forgiven if they defected. Most of the confused peasants left quietly, by twos and threes, while their educated officers and trained sergeants looked on in dismay. Balloons rose around Tokyo telling the enlisted men to think of their families and give up. One of the officers, a captain, put a pistol in his mouth and blew his own brains out. The rest surrendered.

The commissioned officers were given a secret trial, and thirteen of them were executed. Ikki Kita, the folk Christian behind the revolt of 2/26, was also arrested and sentenced to death. He objected only when he was told to kneel for a single bullet in the back of the head. "Hah! So the standing position of Jesus Christ and of Sakura Sogo is no longer to be allowed, eh?"

The February 26 Incident ended in the deaths of the young idealists who had wanted to help the peasants and artisans of Japan enjoy some of the same prosperity that the bankers and industrialists enjoyed. But Hirohito's own people had put him on notice—he was not a popular or respected ruler, and neither the Army nor the people would support him if he knuckled under either to the Russians or to the Western colonialists.

Okada's foreign minister, Koki Hirota, succeeded him as prime minister on March 9. The bright son of a stonemason and a friend of Mitsuru Toyama, head of the Black Dragon Society, he had been adopted by the Hirota family and sent to law school at the Imperial University in Tokyo. His first diplomatic experience had been in the Netherlands, a country he always remembered fondly. He loved to watch the windmills, an ideal example of nature and man in cooperation through simple technology. Hirota served as ambassador to the Soviet Union from 1928 to 1932, where his major accomplishment had been keeping Russia neutral when Japan seized Manchuria and was booted from the League of Nations. Hirota became a strong and consistent anti-communist.

When Hirohito summoned him as prime minister, Hirota protested that the appointment was too great an honor—he may have been serious—but he accepted because nobody else would take the job after the cabinet massacres of 1934 and 1936. He looked at the floor rather than at the emperor as he accepted a mission he himself had proposed—friendship with China, a strong stance against Russia, and a vigilant but friendly relationship with the United States. Hirohito pointedly added a fourth component to Hirota's mission—he was to protect the Japanese nobility against the wrath of the common people. Hirota bowed and accepted the imperial mandate.

During his tenure as prime minister, Hirota—"the man in the ordinary suit," as he called himself, in contrast to the uniformed former generals and admirals who surrounded him in the government—lived in a small house with his wife and children. His idea of a perfect evening was to share a bottle of sake with his half-grown sons. Remembering his own apprenticeship as a stonemason, he liked to watch the carpenters and masons working on new houses in the neighborhood. For nocturnal adventure—he drank at home and had no known mistresses—Hirota might wander out to encourage the neighborhood policemen to squat at their station and play *go*, a Japanese board game. During his service as prime minister, Hirota pursued rural electrification programs, literacy, small manufacturing, vocational education, and the expansion of mandatory public schools for slum and rustic children whose parents could not afford private schools. Hirota tried to fulfill his pledge to protect the nobility by narrowing the yawning gap between the rich and the poor.

Hirota was popular with the poor and the middle classes, and his Black Dragon Society connections enabled him to keep the young officers in line without ducking swords and bullets. His first stumble was diplomatic. Before he assumed office, diplomats in Germany and Japan had begun to work out what came to be called the Anti-Comintern Pact, an alliance of non-communist states against the Soviet Union. Hirota sought an understanding among the major European powers that all of them would resist communism if Stalin moved against any of them. But Shigeru Yoshida, the aristocratic Japanese ambassador to Great Britain, disliked Germany and Italy—upstart powers where the nobility had been marginalized by fascist thugs. Since Germany had already agreed to the alliance, Yoshida made no effort to win over Britain, a country where, in 1936, Hitler still had his upper-class admirers, at least as a bulwark against Russian communism. Hirota himself believed that France, because of its border disputes with Germany, had no place in the alliance. The Anti-Comintern Pact, intended as a barrier against communism, instead became the foundation for the Axis. It was an ironic accomplishment for a working-class statesman who had wanted to foster friendship with China and peace with the United States.

The final act for Hirota's ministry began when Hisaichi Terauchi was appointed war minister less than a year into Hirota's administration. Terauchi was the son of the former governor general of Korea and the World War I prime minister who had rounded up the German colonialists and escorted them out of China and the Mariana Islands. The Army was completing its purges of the 2/26 rebels and soon demanded increasing power in the government. Terauchi, a decorated soldier and son of a war hero, seemed the logical candidate to the militarists. Politicians on both sides dared one another to commit *hara-kiri*, and in the end Hirota resigned. He was replaced by Prince Fumimaro Konoye, a flamboyant relative of the imperial family who had refused the chance to be prime minister when revolution seemed likely. Hirota told friends that all he wanted now was to become a village schoolteacher, but instead he was pressured to become foreign minister— a role for which his friendship with China and his knowledge and suspicion of Russia recommended him.

One month after Konoye took office, the Japanese Army stumbled into a skirmish with Chinese troops near Beijing. The clash itself was farcical, but it set off a chain of events that led to unimaginable tragedy for China, Japan, Asia, and the world.

When the Chinese "Boxers" rose in a murderous rampage against foreign diplomats, missionaries, and Chinese Christian converts in 1900, Japanese troops joined the Western powers in the brutal suppression of the rebellion. Japan shared in the concessions extracted from the prostrate Manchu regime, and in 1937 it still enjoyed the right to police the Japanese-owned railroads that ran through China.

The Japanese had garrisons at several points along the Beijing-Wuhan railroad, including one near the landmark Marco Polo Bridge, southwest of Beijing. On July 7, 1937, a Japanese infantry company was staging night maneuvers in a gravel pit near the bridge. The soldiers set up their machine gun and enlivened the night by firing blanks. They were abruptly splattered with a dozen real bullets from the Chinese garrison stationed nearby, though no one was hit. This incident has never been conclusively explained. Chinese historians have claimed, plausibly, that the Nationalist troops mistook the Japanese blanks for real gunfire. One Japanese historian has asserted that the Chinese fire came from gangsters placed in the Nationalist Army by communists to provoke trouble with the Japanese. In a fight between Chinese anti-communists and Japanese anti-communists, the communists would be the obvious winners. In the confusion of a peacetime unit taking real gunfire, one Japanese enlisted man disappeared. As soon as both sides determined, by telephone calls and personal conversations, that they were not at war, the Japanese asked the Chinese if they had the missing soldier. The Chinese replied that they did not. The missing soldier showed up later that night, alive and unhurt. Accounts differ as to whether he had dropped out of formation to urinate, had slipped away to a brothel, or had fallen into the gravel pit while intoxicated. In any case, he had not been killed or captured by the Chinese. The junior officers on both sides had behaved responsibly. The farce was over. The tragedy was about to begin.

When word of the bloodless gunfire at the Marco Polo Bridge reached the Japanese and Chinese authorities, the hotheads on both sides demanded action. A Japanese airplane accidentally bombed a Chinese barracks manned by puppet troops who were actually in Japanese pay. Believing the bombing to be deliberate, these troops spilled out into a nearby Japanese settlement and murdered 260 Japanese and Koreans. Now that Japanese and Korean blood had been spilled, the Japanese dispatched three divisions to China as reinforcements. The Chinese responded with their own reinforcements. "A war could have started if a Chinese had bumped into a Japanese Army horse," one Japanese statesman said. China and Japan were soon at war.

General Alexander von Falkenhausen, who had left Germany as Hitler rose to power, had been Chiang's military advisor since 1934. By 1937, he was confident that his Prussian training had readied the Nationalist Army to face imperial Japan—a hubristic miscalculation. Falkenhausen and his forty fellow Prussian mercenaries had indeed infused some fight into the youngest and most idealistic of the Nationalist soldiers, brave youngsters of Boy Scout age who showed up in short pants with oversized Mausers and German helmets, ready to build a new future for China. But the peasant and brigand conscripts who filled out the ranks were timid or cynical beyond Falkenhausen's reach.

The first full-scale battle of the Second Sino-Japanese War occurred in August at Shanghai, a notoriously ill-governed city under British or international control, which had the heaviest concentration of prostitutes of any city on earth. Russian women were readily available to men of all races who had money, and Chinese brothels offered pathetic ten-year-old girls who were already addicted to opium. Destitute Chinese fathers offered hapless seven-year-olds in alleys. The Chinese forces amazed everyone by holding out for two months. After the city's fall, men with guns had no trouble satisfying their needs between the fighting. Japanese soldiers began to refer to Chinese women as "public toilets."

In December, the Japanese reached Nanking, the showplace capital of the new China. Nanking was not a whorehouse like Shanghai—the population included large numbers of traditional Chinese people and chaste students at academic institutions. Many of the schools were staffed by Christian missionaries and other Westerners who wanted a better future for China.

Chiang's German advisors told him that Nanking could not be defended, but he let his Army take shelter behind the walls, where many of the undisciplined conscripts made the lives of the Chinese citizens miserable. As the Japanese closed in, Chiang and his command party fled, leaving General Tang Sheng-chih in charge.

"The Chinese command, fully realizing the practical certainty that the Chinese Army would be completely surrounded in the walled city of Nanking—trapped like rats… chose voluntarily to place themselves in just such a situation, apparently with the intention of making the capture of the city as costly to the Japanese as possible in a final heroic gesture of the kind so dear to the Chinese heart," wrote Frank Tillman Durdin, a brave and honest Texan who had covered China for the past seven years as a correspondent for the *New York Times*. "The disgraceful part of the whole business is that the Chinese command proved lacking in the courage needed to carry through their oft-announced and apparent intentions. When Japanese troops had succeeded in breaking over the southwestern wall and while the Hsiakwan back door was still open… General Tang and a few close associates fled, leaving subordinate commanders and well-nigh leaderless troops to the mercy of a hopeless situation, which probably had never been explained to them in the first place."

When the Japanese broke in, those Chinese troops who were still committed to battle turned their own machine guns on the Chinese troops who broke and ran. The Japanese killed the Chinese who fought to the death, and then began to slaughter the military fugitives, some of whom tried to change into clothes they stole from civilians.

"The helpless Chinese troops, disarmed for the most part and ready to surrender, were systematically rounded up and executed," Durdin wrote in a December 18 dispatch. The Japanese had deliberately not shelled the Safety Zone established by Americans and Europeans, but they dragged off many Chinese males of military age they found there and executed them.

"Chinese women were freely molested by Japanese soldiers, and American missionaries personally know of cases where many were taken from refugee camps and violated."

Durdin, respected by both sides for his journalistic integrity, estimated a week after the fall of Nanking that the Chinese Army had lost about thirteen thousand men in battle and another twenty thousand to execution. Japanese casualties were about one thousand. Looting, arson, and rape continued sporadically for the next six weeks. The Japanese military commander, General Iwane Matsui, known as a friend of China in pre-war days, was horrified when he rode his horse into the city in triumph and discovered the carnage and rubble left in the wake of the capture. He angrily rebuked his subordinates, and then his health collapsed and he took to his sickbed. The violence continued for weeks. "There was little glory for either side in the battle of Nanking," Durdin concluded.

There was also little hope that Japan's original intention of uniting and modernizing Asia would survive the documented brutality at Nanking and—perhaps more to the point in political terms—the humiliation that the one-sided battle and the massacre that followed had inflicted on Chiang Kai-shek and his Nationalist government. The Nationalists were now incapable of following their pre-war plan of focusing on Chinese communists and ignoring the seizure of Manchuria. The Chinese then inflated the number of killings at Nanking, and especially the number of rapes, in an attempt to win the sympathy of the American public. Some Americans changed their stance from pro-Japanese to pro-Chinese, while most advocated strict neutrality. Americans sold weapons to one side or the other, or both. The Japanese were now stuck with a war that, militarily, they could not win but that, politically, they could not afford to lose.

Neither revulsion at the Rape of Nanking nor the sinking of the USS *Panay* kept American companies from selling war materiel to the Japanese—and not only steel and gasoline, but aircraft. In 1938, the year after Nanking and the *Panay* incident, Seversky Aircraft Corporation of Farmingdale, New York, accepted an order for twenty two-seater versions of the P-35, then the first-line American fighter plane. These P-35s flew with Japanese pilots at their controls in World War II. For some Americans, the war in China was a business opportunity. Military hardware was sold to both sides until the embargo on selling weapons to any nation but Great Britain was imposed on July 18, 1940.

In 1941, Kajiro Yamamoto released the film *Horse*, one of the great war-time hits. *Horse* is the story of a lovable peasant family who raise a horse as a sort of pet while they raise their children, worry about the horse when it gets sick, and tenderly nurse it back to health. Then the horse is seized as a pack animal for the Japanese Army in China, and the little girl who loves it weeps as it is marched off to the seaport with hundreds of other horses. The metaphor could not be clearer if the film's title were *Son* instead of *Horse*. An assistant on the film was Akira Kurosawa, who would become Japan's greatest director, a man who boasted that he had never handled a gun during the mandatory military training that all Japanese boys had in school. Most Japanese artists, many Japanese men, and virtually all Japanese women thought the war in China was a terrible waste of lives on both sides. The cheering and flag-waving of Hirohito's subjects were a façade. The emperor of Japan ruled a restive country.

CHAPTER 8

THE FINAL COUNTDOWN

Admiral Husband E. Kimmel was appointed to the command of the Pacific Fleet in February 1941 over the heads of thirty-one admirals with more seniority because he was a scrapper: his father, a graduate of West Point, had switched sides during the Civil War in the hope of seeing more action with the Confederate Army than he had seen with the Union Army. Kimmel himself attended Annapolis and served in the Navy. President Roosevelt was not bothered by the Kimmel family history. FDR loved the Navy, but what he loved best was freshly pressed white linen uniforms, snappy salutes, and snappy answers—"The Navy is ready." Admiral Richardson had offended him—"hurt his feelings," as Secretary of the Navy

Frank Knox later told Richardson—by telling him the Navy wasn't ready. The fleet's inadequate antiaircraft batteries, lack of oilers, ammunition ships, and dry docks, second-string fighter planes, and morale problems had clearly indicated to Richardson that his men were not ready for a showdown with the Japanese empire. Roosevelt sacked Richardson for telling him the truth and hoped that Kimmel would be more aggressive. Smedley Butler, a retired Marine general who had twice been awarded the Congressional Medal of Honor, observed in his 1935 book, *War Is a Racket,* that recent U.S. Naval maneuvers looked like an attempt to provoke a war with Japan. Butler would have had no trouble predicting what the administration wanted from Kimmel—assuming that Stanley Hornbeck was wrong about how timid the Japanese were.

Kimmel was on his way back from the golf course near Honolulu when he learned that he was replacing Richardson as commander of the Pacific Fleet. "When I got the news of my prospective assignment I was perfectly stunned," Kimmel wrote to the chief of Naval operations on January 12, 1941. "I hadn't any intimation that Richardson's relief was even being considered... nevertheless, I am prepared to do everything I can when I take over on the first of February." Kimmel said that he did not learn until months later that Richardson had been removed for hurting Roosevelt's feelings. The two friends conferred about the best ways to prepare for what they thought was an attempt to provoke a war with Japan, a war for which both men knew that America was not ready.

When Kimmel took over, one of the first communications he received was a note passed along by Admiral Stark, the chief of Naval operations, based on a telegram sent on January 27 by Ambassador Grew in Japan:

The Peruvian minister has informed a member of my staff that he has heard from many sources, including a Japanese source, that in the event of trouble breaking out between the United States and Japan, the Japanese intend to make a surprise attack on Pearl Harbor with all of their strength and employing all of their equipment. The Peruvian minister considered the rumors fantastic. Nevertheless he considered them of sufficient importance to convey this information to a member of my own staff.

The chief of Naval operations said that he himself placed no credence in the rumors and said that no Japanese move against Pearl Harbor seemed imminent. Kimmel, like Richardson before him, was not so sanguine, since basing the fleet at Pearl Harbor, despite the serious logistical problems involved, was obviously provocative to Japan.

Kimmel, like Richardson—and unlike FDR—knew something about the Japanese military potential. As a young officer he had sailed with the Great White Fleet, which Theodore Roosevelt, generally a friend of Japan, had sent on a round-the-world cruise to show the Japanese that American Naval power was a reality to be reckoned with. Later, he had served with the Asiatic Fleet, based in the Philippines, and he understood America's weakness in the Pacific in comparison with Japan. He noted, among other things, that the single narrow entrance of Pearl Harbor meant that large ships could leave only in single file—a process that took three hours during drills—leaving the fleet vulnerable to the sinking of a single large ship in the channel at the harbor mouth. When Kimmel took command, he only had eleven tankers, and only four of them were capable of refueling his warships while they were under steam on the high seas. The target sleds for gunnery practice had been left on the west coast, and the sleds had to be brought to Hawaii so Kimmel's sailors could learn to handle their guns. On some ships, three out of four men had never been aboard when the guns were fired in practice. Kimmel and his counterpart in the Army, General Walter Short, had asked for a hundred B-17 bombers to patrol the approaches to Pearl Harbor at long range and attack any Japanese invaders from high altitude. They got twelve bombers, six of them generally operable. They also asked for a hundred additional PBY Catalina twin-engine seaplanes for a closer air patrol. They got none. The available Catalina planes had been sent to Britain.

On June 22, 1941, Hitler invaded the Soviet Union. Stalin went into shock, but the NKVD, informed by communist agents in German-occupied Belgium, had been expecting the Nazi onslaught since May. Hitler had postponed the invasion to bail out Mussolini, who had been rebuffed in his invasion of Greece by a very tough Greek Army. The six weeks Hitler wasted helping Mussolini and smashing through politically fragmented Yugoslavia probably cost him the capture of Moscow and Leningrad before winter set in and the Soviets had a chance to organize their vast resources for resistance and counterattack. The Ukrainians—traumatized by Stalin's planned famines and bloody purges of the 1930s—sometimes welcomed the Wehrmacht as liberators. Isolated acts of heroism aside, the Russians themselves put up a very poor fight. The Wehrmacht destroyed six thousand Soviet tanks in one battle and was overwhelmed by Russian prisoners. The British and the Americans expected the Soviet Union to collapse before the end of the year.

Harry Dexter White, the man who had been ordered to protect Stalin's Pacific flank from Japan, was frantic. So was "The Boss,"

Henry Morgenthau Jr., whose abomination of Hitler was based on nobler considerations than White's. Two other figures would play key roles in the buildup to war with Japan. One was Stanley Hornbeck, a strong anti-communist who backed Chiang Kai-shek, and the other was Dean Acheson, a State Department lawyer from an Anglo-Canadian family who saw America's and Britain's interests as not merely compatible but identical. Roosevelt shared Acheson's Anglophilia, though it was tempered by the exigencies of winning reelection in a country where 80 percent of the voters were opposed to war.

None of these men knew that White was a Soviet agent, nor would they have had reason to suspect his communist sympathies. His stated views on economics were moderate and his antipathy to Germany was shared by everyone for obvious reasons. Indeed, White himself may not have been fully conscious of his own treason. To the communist mindset, a communist victory would be a victory for all mankind, and Hitler's savage treatment of the Jews could only have added to that perception in White's case. He was cautious enough, however, to feign conventional patriotism and an unctuous concern for peace with Japan and saving China from both the Japanese and the communists—precisely as Roosevelt, Morgenthau, Hornbeck, and Acheson expected from their people. Yet while Roosevelt and Morgenthau were moneyed lightweights, who got where they were by string-pulling, and Acheson and Hornbeck were ignorant "experts," White actually knew what he was doing. His study of Chinese and Japanese banking and economics had given him to understand that Japan was a political powder magazine where hotheads had killed off a number of senior politicians and where the military's fear of American colonialism was endemic and intense. While everyone else worried about England or the refugees, Harry Dexter White would carry out his mission—to provoke Japan into war with the United States if the United States could not be provoked into war with Japan.

Kimmel received another dispatch from Stark on July 3, which proved prescient:

> The unmistakable deduction from information from numerous sources is that the Japanese Government has determined upon its future policy which is supported by all the principal Japanese political and military groups. This policy probably involves war in the near future. An advance against the British and Dutch cannot be entirely ruled out. However, CNO holds the opinion that Jap activity in the south will be for the present confined to seizure and development of Naval, Army and Air bases in Indo-China.

The dispatch predicted, however, that Japan's target would probably be the maritime provinces of Russia—White's worst nightmare—rather than an attack on the British and the Dutch, which was considered possible but not likely. The United States had responded to the Japanese invasion of Indochina in 1940 with economic sanctions that put Japan in fear for its future supply of oil, prompting the Japanese to negotiate with the Dutch East Indies for a steady oil supply in case of an American cutback. The talks had started on September 10, 1940—a few months after Nazi Germany had conquered the Netherlands and driven the government into exile—and by October the Dutch East Indies had agreed to more than double its exports of oil to Japan, from 570,000 tons annually to 1,800,000 tons. But by December, the Japanese were demanding 3,800,000 tons. The Dutch balked, and American and British diplomats bolstered Dutch resistance to Japan's demands. Expecting a

Japanese incursion into Indochina that summer, Morgenthau—a mouthpiece for White—asked Roosevelt, "What are you going to do on the economic front against Japan if she makes this move?" Roosevelt bluntly told Morgenthau that completely cutting off Japan's oil would provoke a war that Roosevelt did not want and that the Army and Navy did not want either, because they were not ready for it. But Stanley Hornbeck backed economic sanctions, as did Morgenthau (and White).

On July 21, 1941, the Japanese negotiated with the Vichy authorities for control of air and Naval bases in southern Indochina and marched in without a fight. Although Vichy France was allied with Germany, the United States and Britain both reacted to the Japanese incursion by cutting into Japan's credit. The Dutch joined in the embargo. On July 28, a Japanese tanker that showed up at the oil port of Tarakan was sent away empty.

Following his highly developed political instincts, Roosevelt declined an outright embargo. Instead, he authorized a freeze on Japanese assets in the United States that would make it difficult but not impossible for the Japanese to purchase oil. "Now here is this nation called Japan," Roosevelt said in a speech to volunteers from the Office of Civilian Defense,

> Whether they had aggressive purposes to enlarge their empire southward, they did not have any oil of their own. Now, if we had cut the oil off, they probably would have gone down to the Dutch East Indies a year ago, and you would have had war. Therefore, there was—you might call—a method in letting this oil go to Japan, with the hope—and it has worked for two years—of keeping war out of the South Pacific for our own good, for the good of the defense of Great Britain, and the freedom of the seas.

Roosevelt's plan was to require the Japanese to apply for export licenses, but to grant the export licenses as they were applied for—a hindrance to trade but not strangulation. Unfortunately, the granting of the export licenses fell under the jurisdiction of Assistant Secretary of State Dean Acheson, who took it on himself to refuse to release Japanese funds for any purposes at all. Roosevelt's intended slowdown was turned into a *de facto* embargo. Acheson—who probably took Hornbeck's condescending view of Asians much to heart—said that the Japanese would never dare to attack America. What he actually thought is anybody's guess. The president and Secretary of State Hull were both out of town at the time. By the time Roosevelt returned in September, Acheson's embargo was a *fait accompli,* and any reversal might have been construed as weakness. In Japan, Prime Minister Fumimaro Konoye was given a month to get the embargo lifted. Eager for peace and probably in some fear for his life, Konoye invited Ambassador Grew to a private dinner. He offered to meet with Roosevelt at any location of the president's choosing and to agree to any terms that would not bring down the Japanese government.

"I am convinced that he now means business and will go as far as is possible, without incurring open rebellion in Japan, to reach a reasonable understanding with us," Grew wrote to Roosevelt. "It seems to me highly unlikely that this chance will come again."

Roosevelt was reportedly eager to meet with Konoye. Hull and Hornbeck, however, both opposed the meeting, and Roosevelt backed down. The president's reluctance to oppose the State Department in this matter might have been the result, at least in part, of two dispiriting personal losses. In July 1941, his private secretary, Marguerite "Missy" LeHand, collapsed from a stroke at a White House dinner and would never recover. Most historians doubt that Missy LeHand was FDR's mistress, but she assumed most of the roles that the constantly traveling Eleanor would have filled. She meant so much to Roosevelt that in his will he divided his estate evenly between Missy and his wife. He was lost without Missy's day-to-day help. Then on September 7, his beloved and domineering mother, Sara Delano Roosevelt, died just before her eighty-seventh birthday. The president was plunged into a profound private grief that he tried not to let anyone see. He had been excessively dependent on his mother, so much so that Sara sent envelopes of cash to help Eleanor—who fiercely resented her mother-in-law—run the White House. Neither Eleanor nor Franklin had ever depended on a paycheck or knew how to balance a checkbook. When Eleanor sought a divorce after discovering Franklin's love affair with her own social secretary, Lucy Mercer, the iron-willed Sara made it known that a divorce was unthinkable, and there was no divorce. Though the president successfully concealed the depth of this grief at his mother's death, his sadness blunted his resolution.

Roosevelt's relations with the State Department had never been easy. He generally snubbed Cordell Hull, whose appointment as secretary of state was a sop to conservative Southern Democrats. FDR relied so heavily on his old friend Henry Morgenthau Jr. for guidance in international affairs that some people referred to Morgenthau as "the second secretary of state."

Hull's view, recorded in his memoirs, was that Morgenthau "had an excellent organization in the Treasury Department ably led by Harry Dexter White, but he did not stop with his work with the Treasury.... [E]motionally upset by Hitler's rise and his persecution of the Jews, he often sought to induce the President to anticipate the State Department or act contrary to our better judgment." FDR got around Hull's insistence that Morgenthau (and White) keep out of State Department business by relying on his old friend Sumner Welles, an under secretary of state who shared Roosevelt's Groton and Harvard pedigree.

CHAPTER 9

THE NOVEMBER MEMORANDUM

The day before Sara Roosevelt died, the State Department's rebuff of Prime Minister Konoye's urgent request for a private talk with Roosevelt convinced the Japanese to begin serious plans for an attack on Pearl Harbor. At a cabinet meeting on September 6, 1941, Admiral Isoroku Yamamoto was told to attack unless Konoye somehow achieved peace terms with the United States that would not spark a revolution at home, an uprising in Korea, or the restoration of Chinese morale. Hirohito had been shot at twice, once by a Japanese communist, once by a Korean nationalist. The better men of two cabinets had been murdered or wounded because they were seen as too accommodating to the foreigners who wanted to colonize Japan or reduce the nation that had never lost a war in modern times to a vulnerable third-rate power. Konoye himself had been threatened with assassination if he made too many concessions, and there had been serious attempts to overthrow the emperor in favor of his brother or his son. Hirohito knew that his dynasty itself could be wiped out like the Romanovs or marginalized, as the Japanese themselves had done to the Korean royalty, if he bowed to demands that the Japanese saw as not merely insulting but insane.

Yamamoto, who spoke fluent English, had studied at Harvard, and in happier times had hitchhiked across the United States, knew that Japan could not conquer, or even defeat, the United States. The Japanese grand strategy, if war could not be avoided, was to inflict enough damage and seize enough territory that the Americans would guarantee Japanese sovereignty in return for an armistice and restoration of all or most of what Japan had taken outside Korea and perhaps Manchuria.

Theoretical plans for a Japanese attack on Pearl Harbor had existed for decades. General Billy Mitchell had warned as early as 1924 that the next war would be fought with aircraft carriers. The U.S. Navy's Admiral Harry Yarnell conducted a simulated attack by carrier-based aircraft in 1932 as part of a war game. The Navy judges ruled that Pearl Harbor would have sustained substantial damage if the attack had been genuine, and the attackers won the war game.

Yamamoto had delivered his updated contingency plan for an attack on Pearl Harbor on January 7, 1941, less than a month after the British aerial torpedo attack on Taranto. Minoru Genda, Japan's genius of planning, called Yamamoto's initial plan "difficult but not impossible." More information was needed. By the summer of 1941, Korean patriots who kept an ear to the wall at the Japanese consulate in Honolulu through Korean servants and loyal Japanese-Americans were picking up rumors of intense Japanese interest in the depth of water in Pearl Harbor and the strengths and weaknesses of Army and Navy installations in Hawaii.

Roosevelt's restriction on Japan's oil supply shifted Japanese planning into high gear. War was now the only alternative to economic strangulation and political revolution.

On August 10, 1941, Dusko Popov flew on the *Atlantic Clipper* from London to New York. The son of a Yugoslav father and a German mother, Popov was a secret agent for the Abwehr, the German Army's espionage service. He was also an agent for Britain's secret intelligence service, MI6. Popov had despised Hitler even before the Germans invaded Yugoslavia. He now gleefully but covertly accepted salaries and expenses from both German and British intelligence. He was a double agent. Popov—one of the inspirations for the fictional James Bond—spent his fees on the pursuit of actresses, models, and female spies recruited for their sexual allure. Popov's code name was "Tricycle"—not, as some have suggested, because he liked two girls at one time, but because he was the "big wheel" of an espionage team that included another man and a woman as the "little wheels."

Popov's mission from the Abwehr was to bring back a laundry list of data about American military defenses and industrial capacity. His mission from the British—eager to have America in the war and eager for American help should Japan attack British and Dutch colonies—was to tip off the Americans about Japan's sinister interest in Pearl Harbor. In practical terms, Britain was even less ready for a war in the Pacific than the United States was. British propagandists, invoking a crude Darwinism, assured the public that the Japanese would never be formidable airmen—their slanty eyes interfered with peripheral vision, they lost all sense of balance by being carried on their mother's backs as children, and the same lack of imagination that made them fearless foot soldiers made them incapable of becoming quick-thinking pilots. The British had everything to gain, however, by warning the Americans who were supplying much of their military equipment and most of their food, about the possibility of a Japanese surprise attack on Pearl Harbor.

Popov was initially unable to gain an audience with J. Edgar Hoover, the director of the FBI, who did not like British intelligence operating in the United States or Popov's playboy reputation. To the FBI agent who met him at the Waldorf Astoria in New York City, Popov showed off a newly invented German microdot technology by which hundreds of words could be printed in the space of a period. Then, with the knowledge of MI6 but not of the Abwehr, Popov handed the agent an English translation of the Japanese request for information about Pearl Harbor and the Abwehr's request for military and economic information.

The MI6 translation of the Abwehr list was two pages long, and Pearl Harbor dominated the first page:

Hawaii—ammunition dumps and mine depots.

Details about Naval ammunition and mine depot on the Isle of Kushua [sic] (Pearl Harbour). If possible sketch.

Naval ammunition depot Lualuelei, Exact position. Is there a railway line [junction]?

The total ammunition reserve of the Army is supposed to be in the rock of the crater Aliamanu. Position?

Is the Crater Punchbowl [Honolulu] being used as ammunition dump? If not, are there other military works?

Aerodromes.

Aerodrome Lukefield—details. Sketch (if possible.) regarding the situation of the hangars (number?) workshops, bomb depots, and petrol depots. Are there underground petrol installations?—Exact position of the seaplane station? Occupation?

Naval air arm strong point Kaneche—Exact report regarding position, number of hangars, depots and workshops. [sketch] Occupation?

Army aerodromes Wicham [sic] Field and Wheeler Field—Exact position? Reports regarding exact number of hangars, depots and workshops. Underground installations? [Sketch].

Rodger's Airport—in case of war, will this place be taken over by the Army or the Navy? What preparations have been made? Number of hangars? Are there landing possibilities for seaplanes?

Airport of the Panamerican airways.—Exact position? (If possible sketch.) Is this airport possibly identical with Rodger's Airport or a part thereof? (A wireless station of the Panamerican Airways is on the Peninsula Mohapuu.)

Naval Strong Point Pearl Harbour

Exact details and sketch about the situation of the state wharf, of the pier installations, workshops, petrol installations, situations of dry dock No. 1 and of the new dry dock which is being built.

Details about the submarine station (plan of situation). What land installations are in existence?

Where is the station for mine search formations [*Minensuchverbände*]? How far has the dredge work progressed at the entrance and in the east and southeast lock? Depth of water?

Number of anchorages. [*Liegeplätze*]?

Is there a floating dock in Pearl Harbour or is the transfer of such a dock to this place intended?

Special tasks.—Reports about torpedo protection nets newly introduced in the British and U.S.A. Navy. How far are they already in existence in the merchant and Naval fleet? Use during voyage? Average speed reduction when in use. Details of construction and others.

The second page of the list contained questions of more interest to the German Army, then fighting the British for North Africa, than to the Japanese Navy, but the whole first page, minus the introductory paragraph, was a request for military data about Pearl Harbor.

Popov, who had supplied this storm warning of a serious Japanese interest in attacking Pearl Harbor, was kept cooling his heels in New York City for two weeks. When Hoover finally came from Washington to see him, he insulted Popov as a sex-crazed scoundrel and threatened to have him arrested for violation of the Mann Act. (The woman in question was a British national and very much a consenting adult. Popov soon abandoned her for Simone Simon, a French actress then making a film in America.) Popov had hoped to follow his usual practice—visit Hawaii and send the Abwehr a few fragments of good information along with whatever misinformation MI6 or the FBI wanted the Abwehr to receive. He never got permission to visit Hawaii. From the German-Japanese viewpoint, Popov's mission was a dismal failure.

Popov's list of questions clearly indicated that Pearl Harbor was the key target. It also indicated that the attack would be primarily by air rather than Naval bombardment and would involve both bombs (the Punchbowl question) and torpedoes (the torpedo net question and the anchorage question). Common sense suggested that the American aircraft would be neutralized at the outset and that the Japanese would attempt to destroy the oil tanks as well as the dry docks needed for repairs. The only information missing was the date. When Popov dropped off the Abwehr document in August, the Japanese were still hoping for terms that would head off a war.

Meanwhile, after Popov's failure to reach Hawaii, the Japanese were doing their homework. The Japanese diplomats in Egypt made a habit of eavesdropping on Admiral Andrew Browne Cunningham, the commander in chief of the British Mediterranean fleet, and of drinking with some of his junior officers. The Japanese learned the secret of success in the torpedo attack on the Italian fleet at Taranto. The British had fitted their aerial torpedoes with wooden stabilizer fins to arrest their plunge when they were dropped and wooden nose-caps that broke away and armed the torpedoes during the short run to their target. The British had helped to build the Japanese Navy in the nineteenth century. Now their improvised aerial torpedoes would help to sink a large part of the American Navy in the twentieth.

Japanese Naval officer candidates had to pass rigorous swimming tests. The Japanese sent some of these good swimmers to chart the depths around Battleship Row, Ford Island, and the rest of Pearl Harbor. Fishing boats provided depth data for the open sea near Oahu. The autumn of 1941 found the Japanese in possession of a detailed oceanographic picture of the defenses of Hawaii around Honolulu.

Fumimaro Konoye, who attended costume parties dressed alternately as a geisha and as Adolf Hitler, was fond of flamboyant gestures. But Konoye knew that Japan could not hope to win a war with the United States. At the same time, he knew that pulling the Japanese Army out of China would invite his assassination and perhaps touch off a revolution against the emperor, whom they were sworn to defend.

On the American side, those who wanted peace in the Pacific— Ambassador Grew, the president, and most of the State Department—were undermined by Dean Acheson and Stanley Hornbeck, who both expected the Japanese to capitulate. Harry Dexter White and his puppet Morgenthau wanted war and were prepared to push all the necessary buttons. The secretary of war, Henry Stimson, also favored a tough stance with Japan, but the serving soldiers—General Marshall in Washington and Admiral Kimmel at Pearl Harbor—knew that America was not equipped for war. The high-performance P-38 fighter plane, the M-1 semiautomatic rifle, the Sherman tank, and the all-important 20-millimeter and

Harry Dexter White, 1892–1948
(*INTERNATIONAL MONETARY FUND*).

TOP: "Two of a Kind": Henry Morgenthau Jr. and Franklin D. Roosevelt *(WIKIMEDIA COMMONS)*. **OPPOSITE (top):** Iskhak "Bill" Akhmerov, the NKVD agent who recruited Harry Dexter White. **OPPOSITE (center):** Whittaker Chambers, the Soviet courier whom Harry Dexter White knew only as "Carl" *(WIKIMEDIA COMMONS)*. **OPPOSITE (bottom):** Vitalii Pavlov, Harry Dexter White's NKVD lunch date at Washington's Old Ebbitt Grill.

two of a kind

_____ Roosevelt

TOP (left): Admiral James Richardson greets Admiral Kichisaburo Nomura, Japan's new ambassador, who stopped at Pearl Harbor en route to Washington, January 1941 (U.S. NAVY). TOP (right): Rebel troops in the February 26 Incident, Tokyo, 1936. BOTTOM: Rebel troops guard police headquarters in the February 26 Incident, Tokyo, 1936. OPPOSITE: Hirohito, the uneasy occupant of Japan's imperial throne.

TOP: The horrifying success of Operation Snow: the USS *Arizona* in flames at Pearl Harbor *(LIBRARY OF CONGRESS)*. LEFT: Dean Acheson, State Department mastermind of the U.S. oil embargo against Japan *(WIKIMEDIA COMMONS)*. BOTTOM (left): Koki Hirota, son of a stonemason and "the man in the ordinary suit." As prime minister, he pursued an anticommunist policy and peace with the United States *(WIKIMEDIA COMMONS)*. BOTTOM (right): Prince Fumimaro Konoye. When Hull and Hornbeck scuttled his urgent bid for a meeting with FDR, he was replaced as prime minister and Japan headed to war *(WIKIMEDIA COMMONS)*.

TOP (left): Kilsoo Haan, the Korean patriot who warned Washington of the very date of the attack *(AMERICAN HERITAGE CENTER, UNIVERSITY OF WYOMING)*. **TOP (right):** Admiral Husband E. Kimmel, commander in chief of the U.S. Pacific Fleet and the Roosevelt administration's chief scapegoat *(ASSOCIATED PRESS)*. **BOTTOM:** General Georgi Zhukov, Red Army commander at Nomonhan *(RUSSIAN INTERNATIONAL NEWS AGENCY, WORLD WAR II DATABASE)*.

TOP: Ambassador Nomura, Secretary of State Hull, and Special envoy Kurusu meet on the eve of the war *(ASSOCI-ATED PRESS)*. **CENTER:** U.S. delegation to the Bretton Woods Conference. HDW, back row, far left; Dean Acheson, back row, 3rd from left; Henry Morgenthau Jr., front row, 2nd from right *(©BETTMANN/CORBIS/APIMAGES)*. **BOTTOM:** Harry Dexter White testifies before the House Un-American Activities Committee, August 13, 1948. Three days later he was dead *(ASSOCIATED PRESS)*.

40-millimeter antiaircraft guns had been ordered but were not yet in general issue and would not be ready until the middle of 1942 or later. Even the Jeep was in short supply in the autumn of 1941. Soldiers and sailors still wore pie-pan tin hats instead of the deep-dish helmets that would serve the American G.I. through Vietnam, and they carried bolt-action 1903 Springfield rifles with a slower rate of fire than the Winchesters and Henrys that the Lakota and Cheyenne wielded at Little Big Horn. The standard machine gun was water-cooled and weighed almost one hundred pounds. The standard U.S. tank had a 37-millimeter gun that bounced off German armor without piercing and threw its treads in a sharp turn. The generals urged the diplomats to stall for time.

The Japanese generals urged their own diplomats to temporize, even though they came to see war as inevitable unless the Americans restored the oil supply in return for concessions that the junior officers and the common people would tolerate. Ambassador Nomura handed the U.S. State Department Japan's offer for a stand-down on September 6:

The government of Japan undertakes:

(a) that Japan is ready to express its concurrence in those matters which were already tentatively agreed upon between Japan and the United States in the course of their preliminary informal conversations;

(b) that Japan will not make any military advancement from French Indochina against any of its adjoining areas, and likewise will not, without any justifiable reason, resort to any military action against any regions lying south of Japan [that is, the British, Dutch, and American colonies—Malaya, Indonesia, and the Philippines];

(c) that the attitudes of Japan and the United States towards the European War will be decided by the concepts of protection and self-defense, and, in case the United States should participate in the European War, the interpretation and execution of the Tripartite Pact by Japan shall be independently decided;

(That is to say, Japan did not feel obliged to join Germany and Italy if the European Axis declared war on the United States. The Japanese had assisted the British against the Germans during World War I, mopping up Germany's Pacific garrisons and escorting Australian and New Zealand troops to Europe. Japan had no part in Hitler's vicious hatred of Jews and had accepted tens of thousands of Jewish refugees. Indeed, the Japanese rather liked the French, had been loyal allies of the British, and, as mentioned previously, tended to sentimentalize the United States as a land of marriage for love. Japan's allegiance to the Axis had only one basis: anti-communism.)

(d) that Japan will endeavor to bring about the rehabilitation of general and normal relationship between Japan and China, upon the realization of which Japan is ready to withdraw its armed forces from China as soon as possible in accordance with the agreements between Japan and China.

This was the key concession: Japan was willing to get out of China—though not Manchuria—as soon as the Chinese agreed to an armistice. For most Americans, including Cordell Hull, and for Chinese propagandists, the history of Sino-Japanese relations began with the Rape of Nanking. Before Hirohito's accession, however, Japanese progressives had courageously supported Chinese liberators like Sun Yat-sen. Chiang Kai-shek himself had studied in Japan, as had thousands of other Chinese. Japan had seized Manchuria for crass economic reasons, but by 1941 the Japanese knew they would not conquer the rest of China and were looking for a way out of an increasingly unpopular war.

Instead of leaping at Japan's offer to back out of its war with China and its tacit dismissal of its alliance with Nazi Germany, Hull, relying on Hornbeck, pronounced the proposal vague and unacceptable. On September 15, the United States—which could read Japan's encoded diplomatic cables—intercepted a message from Nomura to Konoye that terminated hopes of a meeting between the prime minister and Roosevelt:

> Whatever we tell to Secretary Hull you should understand will surely be passed on to the President if he is in Washington. It seems that the matter of preliminary conversations has been entrusted by the President to Secretary Hull, in fact he told me that if a matter could not by settled by me and Secretary Hull it would not be settled whoever conducted the conversations. Hull himself told me that during the past eight years he and the President had not differed on foreign policies once, and that they are as "two in one."

Hull's representation to Nomura of his relationship with the president was, of course, preposterous. Hull's resentment of Roosevelt's reliance on Morgenthau and Welles was palpable, and it probably sabotaged Konoye's desperate grab for peace.

Konoye's peace proposal was dead on arrival. At Konoye's final cabinet meeting, the war minister, General Hideki Tojo, summed up the disgrace of Konoye's failure and the further danger of any more concessions to the predatory Americans. "The heart of the matter is the imposition on us of withdrawal from Indochina and China.... If we yield to America's demands, it will destroy the fruits of the [Second Sino-Japanese war]. Manchukou [Manchuria] will be endangered and our control of Korea undermined." On October 16, the cabinet was dismissed and Konoye was replaced by Tojo, the future scapegoat.

After the war, when Konoye had attempted suicide and Tojo, who had failed in his suicide attempt, had been hanged for war crimes, Americans reinvented Japanese history. Konoye the peaceful, so the story went, had been pushed aside by Tojo the militarist. In fact, Konoye had given up in despair when Roosevelt declined to meet with him or to accept the best terms that Konoye could offer without provoking a rebellion at home. Tojo had planned no militarist takeover. He was a rather modest man, known for his vast respect for the emperor and more famous for his memory for detail than for any vision or brilliance. His nickname was *kamisori*—the razor—because he could sort out details of careers and promotions more quickly than most of his peers. His parents were not nobles or high-ranking samurai, though his father had become a lieutenant general through sheer diligence, and his own grades were respectably mediocre. Tojo owed everything to the imperial system and the Army. His most important qualities were humility and loyalty. Though he had three sons and four daughters, he reached into his own pocket to help friends in need. His house in the Tokyo neighborhood of Setagaya-ku was respectable but ordinary, and his wife and children were decent, likable people without pretensions. Tojo was the perfect helmsman for the ship of state as it sailed into a war it could not win—and the emperor knew it.

Tojo himself was so modest that when he was summoned to the palace, he thought the emperor was about to rebuke him and prepared to abase himself. When he was asked to become prime minister in place of Konoye, he tried at first to refuse but eventually accepted out of devotion to the emperor and the system that had made him a general instead of a craftsman or farmer.

"I don't know much about Tojo as a man," the former prime minister Koki Hirota, "the man in the ordinary suit," told his sons Hiroo and Masao just after Tojo's appointment. "However, it seems that he listens to what the lord privy seal has to say.... [B]y now, a pure figurehead would only do more harm. The Army will have to take responsibility itself. If he's put in a position where he has no choice but to get the Army to agree to holding diplomatic negotiations, Tojo isn't likely to do anything too rash."

The Tojo cabinet announced that negotiations with the United States would continue but urged the Americans to be willing to make some concessions. The State Department interpreted this to mean that the Japanese war lords intended to continue their expansionist policies—after Konoye had offered to back out of China and had been rebuffed.

Both sides temporized—temporarily. Japan was not ready for a long war; it lacked manpower, oil, iron, aluminum, and food. America, which lagged behind Japan in fighter planes and warships, was also not ready for a war within the next six months. Then, while the Americans were trying to castigate the Japanese war lords for their aggressive posture, an astonishing spread appeared in the October 31 issue of *United States News* (the predecessor of *U.S. News & World Report*), showing just how easy it would be for United States B-17 bombers to blow Japan off the map in case of trouble.

Japan is today within range of bomber attacks from seven main points. Bases at those points are being kept at wartime strength and readiness by the United States, Britain, China and Russia.

In airline miles, distances from the bases to Tokyo are as follows: Unalaska—2,700; Guam—1,575; Cavite, P.I.—1,860; Singapore—3,250; Hongkong—1,825; Chungking—2,000; Vladivostock—440.

Comparable figures for flying time from the bases are shown by the Pictogram. These figures are based on the use of a bomber with a flying range of 6,000 miles and an average speed of 250 miles an hour, a type representative of those to be turned out on a large scale for American air forces and for shipment to Britain and China.

Principal targets for enemy bombers attacking Japan would be the Tokyo-Yokohama area and the city of Osaka, 240 miles southward. These two areas are the head and the heart of industrial Japan.

Tokyo, city of rice-paper and wood houses, is the center of transportation, government and commerce. Only 15 miles away is Yokohama, home base of the Japanese Navy. Damage to the repair and supply facilities there would seriously cripple the fleet, Japan's main striking force.

At Osaka is concentrated most of the national munitions industry. Hastily expanded during the last three years, the arms factories are built of wood. Acres upon acres of these wooden buildings in and near the city present a highly vulnerable target for incendiary bombs. This same strategic liability is true of other cities, making it imperative to keep attacking planes at a distance. Use of aircraft carriers by hostile forces would intensify the difficulty of this task for the Japanese Navy and air force.

These facts influence the decision of Japan's leaders today. And the facts are made ever more pointed for them by the spectacle of American-produced bombers, aviation gasoline and supplies flowing into Vladivostok, nearest source of danger to their capital.

This article, published on Halloween, was a lurid fantasy. U.S. B-17s did not have the range to reach most of Japan and return to the Philippines, and the desperate Russians battling Hitler at the gates of Moscow and Leningrad had no plans to invite a Japanese attack by allowing Americans to land in Vladivostok. But the Japanese probably did not know that. A major U.S. magazine had proposed American incendiary attacks on Japanese cities—five weeks before Pearl Harbor.

Chiang Kai-shek, the generalissimo who had told his unpaid soldiers to fight to the death for Nanking and had then run out on them, must have seen the article, because he started to ask the United States for more aircraft and an ultimatum to Japan. The State Department passed the request on to the War Department and the Navy Department. The professional military men knew that money sent to Chiang was more likely to go for bribes than for bullets or bombs. On November 5 the memo came back from Chief of Staff George Marshall and Secretary of the Navy Frank Knox:

[T]he dispatch of United States armed forces for intervention in China against Japan is disapproved.

> ... [m]aterial aid to China [should] be accelerated
> consistent with the needs of Russia, Great Britain, and
> our own forces.
>   ... that aid to the American Volunteer Group (*the
> Flying Tigers*) be continued and accelerated to the max-
> imum practicable extent.
>   ...that no ultimatum be delivered to Japan.

Chiang was told on November 14 not to expect American troops
or aircraft. The next day, General Marshall held a confidential press
conference where the possibility of bombing Japanese civilians in
case of war was once again discussed—this time before reporters
who were pledged to silence, though Marshall himself confirmed
the interview. Marshall—who may have been the source for the
story in *United States News*—said that America would use the
threat of bombing to keep Japanese "fanatics" peaceful, but that
the bombings would be carried out in case of war.

"We'll fight mercilessly," Marshall said. "Flying Fortresses
[B-17s] will be dispatched immediately to set the paper cities of
Japan on fire.... [T]here won't be any hesitation about bombing
civilians—it will be all out."

Even as Marshall spoke, B-17s were being sent to defend the
Philippines, if not to prepare for the threatened destruction of
Japanese paper cities. These were the same B-17s that Admiral
Richardson and Admiral Kimmel had urgently but unsuccessfully
requested for long-range reconnaissance around Hawaii to protect
Pearl Harbor.

On November 15, as Ambassador Grew, the most pro-Japanese
diplomat in the State Department, was warning the United States
to expect a Japanese surprise attack if negotiations were not concluded, Saburo Kurusu arrived as a special envoy on an emergency

visit to Washington. "Daddy" Kurusu, known to Japanese diplomats as a kindly father figure, fluent in English and married to an American, joined Nomura on a visit to the White House two days later. Kurusu told Roosevelt and Hull that the Tojo government continued to hope for peace. Unfortunately, Kurusu was the signer of the Anti-Comintern Pact with Hitler and Mussolini. Hull lectured Kurusu and Nomura about the alliance with Hitler—the alliance that Konoye had indicated Japan would let slide in case Germany attacked the United States.

"I made it clear," Hull recalled, "that any kind of a peaceful settlement for the Pacific areas, with Japan still clinging to her Tripartite Pact with Germany, would cause the President and myself to be denounced in immeasurable terms and the peace arrangement would not for a moment be taken seriously while all of the countries interested in the Pacific would redouble their efforts to arm against Japanese aggression. I emphasized the point about the Tripartite Pact and self-defense by saying that when Hitler starts on a march of invasion across the earth with ten million soldiers and thirty thousand airplanes with an official announcement that he is out for unlimited invasion objectives, this country from that time was in danger and that danger has grown each week until this minute."

The Japanese listened to Hull's fantasies about Hitler's taking over the United States, appalled at his lack of information about Nazi Germany's actual military potential. The Germans had no four-engine bombers except for a few converted airliners used as long distance patrol planes. Their best battleship, the *Bismarck*, had been surrounded and sunk by the British in May 1941. The Wehrmacht had failed to cross the twenty-mile-wide English Channel in 1940 despite temporary air supremacy. Did Hull really expect the Germans to take on the British and American Navies at the same time and then ferry troops three thousand miles across the Atlantic when they were already badly over-committed in Russia, North Africa, and the Balkans?

The following day, Hull—the statesman who would not accept German-Jewish refugees when their ship was stuck in a Cuban harbor—delivered to the Japanese, who had accepted forty thousand Jewish refugees, another lecture about Nazi atrocities. Maintaining their composure, Kurusu and Nomura proposed a *modus vivendi*—a temporary solution until a permanent agreement could be reached. Though suspicious of Hull's grip on reality and his palpable racism, the Japanese diplomats acted in good faith because they did not want war any more than Marshall and Knox did. They agreed to pull out of southern Indochina as soon as their oil was restored and to leave Indochina completely once peace was made with China. In return,

> The Governments of Japan and the United States shall cooperate with a view to securing the acquisition of those goods and commodities which the two countries need in the Netherlands East Indies.
>
> The Governments of Japan and the United States mutually undertake to restore their commercial relations to those prevailing prior to the freezing of the assets [on July 26]. The Government of the United States shall supply Japan a required quantity of oil.
>
> The Government of the United States undertakes to refrain from such measures and actions as will be prejudicial to the endeavors for the restoration of general peace between Japan and China.

Both sides stood to gain: Japan could not win a protracted war with the United States, and most Japanese wanted to get out of

China with minimum loss of face, while keeping Manchuria and Korea and fending off revolution. The U.S. would avoid a war for which it was not prepared. Even Chiang Kai-shek, for all his hurt pride, would have been better off to strike an armistice with Japan and go back to fighting the Chinese communists. To everybody's amazement—perhaps even his own—Hull replied that he would see what actions on Japan's part would be necessary for the flow of oil to be restored.

Harry Dexter White was badly shaken. The possibility that Hull, Morgenthau's adversary, would head off a war with Japan just when everything seemed so promising was utterly vexing. Writing frantically through the night, despite an incipient heart condition, White composed for Morgenthau's signature a memorandum to the president proposing a set of demands so likely, if accepted, to incite revolution in Japan that their rejection would be assured.

> I must apologize for intruding on your pressing schedule with this hurried note. I have been so alarmed by information reaching me last night—information which I hope and trust to be mistaken—that my deep admiration for your leadership in world affairs forces me respectfully to call your attention to the matter that has kept me from sleep last night.
>
> Mr. President, word was brought to me yesterday evening that persons in our country's government are hoping to betray the cause of the heroic Chinese people and strike a deadly blow at all your plans for a world-wide democratic victory. I was told that the Japanese Embassy staff is openly boasting of a great triumph for the "New Order." Oil—rivers of oil—will

soon be flowing to the Japanese war machines. A humiliated democracy of the Far East, China, Holland, Great Britain will soon be facing a Fascist coalition emboldened and strengthened by diplomatic victory—so the Japanese are saying.

Mr. President, I am aware that many honest individuals agree that a Far East Munich is necessary at the moment. But I write this letter because millions of human beings everywhere in the world share with me the profound conviction that you will lead a suffering world to victory over the menace to all of our lives and all of our liberties. To sell China to her enemies for the thirty blood-stained coins of gold will not only weaken our national policy in Europe as well as the Far East, but will dim the bright luster of America's world leadership in the great democratic fight against Fascism.

On this day, Mr. President, the whole country looks to you to save America's power as well as her sacred honor. I know—I have the most perfect confidence—that should these stories be true, should there be Americans who seek to destroy your declared policy in world affairs, that you will succeed in circumventing these plotters of a new Munich.

White held nothing back in this hysterical missive, mingling religious imagery (inaccurately at that—Christ was betrayed for thirty pieces of *silver*) with the basest flattery.

The next night, White wrote a second memorandum, this time under his own name. He opened with the assurance that, if the president were to follow his advice and if the Japanese were to accept his proposals, "the whole world would be electrified by the successful transformation of a threatening and belligerent powerful enemy into a peaceful and prosperous neighbor. The prestige and the leadership of the President both at home and abroad would skyrocket by so brilliant and momentous a diplomatic victory—a victory that requires no vanquish, a victory that immediately would bring peace, happiness and prosperity to hundreds of millions of Eastern peoples, and assure the subsequent defeat of Germany!" White pointed out the hopelessness of a Japanese war against the United States, Britain, the Netherlands, and probably Russia while Japan was already engaged in China. Then he proposed ten aggressive demands to be presented to Japan:

1. Withdraw all military, Naval, air police forces from China (boundaries as of 1931), from Indo-China and from Thailand.
2. Withdraw all support—military, political, or economic—from any government in China other than that of the national government. [This referred to Pu Yi, the last Manchu emperor of China, who was the Japanese puppet ruler in Manchukuo, Japan's colony in Manchuria.]
3. Replace with yen currency at a rate agreed upon among the Treasuries of China, Japan, England, and United States all military scrip, yen and puppet notes circulating in China.
4. Give up all extra-territorial rights in China.
5. Extend to China a billion yen loan at 2 percent to aid in reconstructing China (at a rate of 100 million yen a year).
6. Withdraw all Japanese troops from Manchuria except for a few divisions necessary as a police force, provided U.S.S.R. withdraws all her troops from the Far Eastern front except for an equivalent remainder.

7. Sell to the United States up to three-fourths of her current output of war material—including Naval, air, ordnance, and commercial ships on a cost-plus 20 per cent basis as the United States may select.
8. Expel all German technical men, military officials, and propagandists.
9. Accord the United States and China most-favored-nation treatment in the whole Japanese Empire.
10. Negotiate a 10-year non-aggression pact with United States, China, British Empire, Dutch Indies (and Philippines).

White proposed that these demands be presented to the Japanese with a short deadline for acceptance:

> Inasmuch as the United States cannot permit the present uncertain status between the United States and Japan to continue in view of world developments, and feels that decisive action is called for now, the United States should extend the above offer of a generous and peaceful solution of the difficulties between the two countries for only a limited time. If the Japanese Government does not indicate its acceptance in principle at least of the proffered terms before the expiration of that time, it can mean only that the present Japanese Government prefers other and less peaceful ways of solving those difficulties, and is awaiting the propitious moment to attempt to carry out further a plan of conquest.

Japanese industrial interests and the Army were certain to reject the loss of Manchuria, and the idea that Japan should be forced to sell three-quarters of its military equipment to the United States on demand was an affront to Japanese sovereignty that would have triggered revolution. White passed a copy of the memorandum along to Hull, who had been considering a three-month truce and limited oil shipments for Japanese civilian consumption.

On November 26, the secretary of state presented the final American offer—the so-called "Hull note"—to the Japanese. If Japan withdrew from China and Indochina immediately and withdrew support for the puppet regime in Manchukuo, the United States would lift the freeze on Japanese assets. When he received the offer, Kurusu stated that the Japanese would be likely to "throw up their hands" at the demand that they withdraw from China and abandon Manchuria. The Hull note—based on White's two memoranda—was, as far as the Japanese were concerned, a declaration of war.

The Americans did not see it that way—except for White.

"I personally was relieved," Henry Stimson would recall, "that we had not backed down on any of the fundamental principles on which we had stood for so long and which I felt we could not give up without the sacrifice of our national honor and prestige in the world. I submit, however, that no impartial reading of this document can characterize it as being couched in the terms of an ultimatum, although the Japanese were of course only too quick to seize upon it and give that designation for their own purposes."

The day after the Hull note was delivered, Stanley Hornbeck, who had helped draft it, based on White's memorandum, wrote in a memorandum of his own, "The Japanese government does not desire or intend or expect to have forthwith armed conflict with the United States.... Were it a matter of placing bets, the undersigned would give odds of five to one that Japan and the United States will not be at 'war' on or before March 1 (a date more than

90 days from now, and after the period during which it has been estimated by our strategists that it would be to our advantage for us to have 'time' for further preparation and disposals)."

When the news of the American ultimatum reached Tokyo, the Japanese were horrified. Foreign Minister Togo tried to resign. The emperor, groping for a way to save his throne and perhaps his life without war, called a meeting of Japan's former prime ministers. One by one, the weary old men, fearful for their country if not for their own lives, appeared before the emperor to try to find a way to avoid a revolution at home or destruction at the hands of America or Russia.

Reijiro Wakatsuki, born in 1866, a lawyer known as "the liar" in a pun on his name, had become prime minister for a second time after his predecessor, Hamaguchi, was critically wounded in an assassination attempt. He had unsuccessfully opposed the annexation of Manchuria. His position was that the war with the United States could not be prevented given America's impossible demands, but that the Japanese should try to end hostilities as quickly as possible.

Keisuke Okada, born in 1868, the prime minister who had escaped by hiding in the toilet on February 26, 1936, knew only too well what would happen if the cabinet bowed to the foreigners. He had no answer to America's demands either.

Kiichiro Hiranuma, born in 1867, was a reformer who had made his name prosecuting corrupt monopolies and the politicians who accepted their bribes. A nationalist and an anti-communist, he had resigned in 1939 because he feared that Japan's developing alliance with Germany would draw his country into an unwanted war with Britain and the United States. Hiranuma also understood that giving up Manchuria under American pressure was political suicide.

Mitsumasa Yonai, born in 1880, an admiral nicknamed "the white elephant" because of his pale skin and large ears and nose, had just avoided assassination on February 26, 1936. He was visiting his mistress at her home when the death squad showed up at his office. Yonai was pro-British and pro-American and had opposed the alliance with Hitler. Despite his narrow escape in 1936, Yonai thought that the Japanese should risk popular outrage one more time: "I hope the nation will not jump from the frying pan into the fire."

Koki Hirota, "the man in the ordinary suit," came next. He asked the cabinet to consider that a diplomatic breakdown might not lead to war. He doubted that America would go to war for the sake of China and said that, in any case, the Japanese should look for a peace settlement as quickly as possible if war broke out. None of these elder statesmen could suggest an offer to the United States that might ameliorate its drastic and startling demands. They were baffled by a once-friendly country that had, until recently, been selling them not only oil and scrap iron but military training aircraft and spare parts. Roosevelt, for whatever reason, seemed to have lost all interest in avoiding war in the Pacific and had left Hull, Hornbeck, and White minding the store.

On December 1, the emperor met with his privy council. "It is now clear that Japan's claims cannot be attained through diplomatic means," Tojo said. The emperor—perhaps more gun-shy than the elder statesmen—asked for a vote. The cabinet voted unanimously for war. Hirohito agreed. The Japanese fleet was told to attack Pearl Harbor on December 7 unless it received a last-minute cancellation because of a sudden change in America's attitude. Kurusu and Nomura—who had been sincere in seeking peace until they received the Hull note—were told to stall for time. Tojo summed up the situation: Japan, the one Asian, African, or

CHAPTER 10

THE KOREAN CASSANDRA

A young Korean American would often drop into my office. He was in touch with the anti-Japanese underground in Korea. Pearl Harbor, he would tell me, before Christmas. He could get no audience at the State Department.
—Eric Sevareid

August 29, 1941
President Franklin D. Roosevelt
White House
Washington, D.C.
Dear Mr. President Roosevelt:

As one who represents the Korean Underground in America; as the one who on January 8, 1941 wrote you from Los Angeles, California the information contained in Japan's war plan book, *Three Power Alliance and the US-Japanese War*, that at the opening of the US-Japanese War, Japan will call for peace negotiations and during these peace talks, Japan is to carry-out the surprise attack upon Pearl Harbor, Hawaii, may I sincerely appeal to you not to trust the Japanese Ambassador Nomura?

I have learned that in July your excellency, Mr. President had proposed to Nomura that America and England will supply Japan's need of oil, gasoline, scrap irons and essential food supplies if Japan get out of French Indo China and acknowledge the neutrality of French Indo China.

As long ago as April 1933 I informed Secretary of War Dern [George Dern, Roosevelt's first secretary of war], the US-Japan War is inevitable hence the July proposal by Mr. President to Ambassador Nomura is of no use to America, where as it will encourage the Japanese Emperor and his military advisors to implement Japan's war plan the surprise attack on Hawaii.

Please cease fooling yourself and be prepared for war.

Respectfully,
Kilsoo Haan

Kilsoo Haan was a man who loved two countries, the United States and Korea, and hated one, Japan. Based in Washington, D.C., in the autumn of 1941, he had the ear of several statesmen, including Senator Guy Gillette of Iowa. Haan attempted at least eight times to warn the United States of an impending attack on Pearl Harbor. There were many indications, including newspaper headlines, that a war with Japan was about to break out, but Haan consistently predicted a surprise attack on Hawaii on the first weekend of December for at least four months before the attack took place.

Oct. 28, 1941
Hon. Henry L. Stimson
Secretary of War
Information

I am at the request of my agent submitting this information sent to me from the Orient, dated Aug. 26, 1941. A copy will be sent to the State Department, Cordell Hull.

Information: Hirota, former foreign minister, now the "big stick" of the Black Dragon Society, in their Aug. 26 meeting, told of the news that war minister Tojo has ordered a total war preparation to meet the armed forces of the United States in this Pacific emergency. Tojo is said to have told him of the Navy's full support of his policy against America.

He also spoke of Tojo giving orders to complete the mounting of guns and rush supplies of munitions to the Marshall and Caroline group (mandated islands) by November 1941. Hirota and others present in the meeting freely discussed and expressed opinions as to the advantages and consequences of a war with America. Many expressed the most suitable time to wage war with America is Dec. 1941 or Feb. 1942. Many said:

"Tojo (now Premier) will start the war with America and after 60 days Tojo will reshuffle the cabinet and become virtually a great dictator."

Note: based on this information dated Aug. 26, 1941, Japan's recent and sudden change of cabinet is a planned one, stalling for time for closer collaboration and more effective cooperation in the interest of the Axis Powers.

Mounting of guns and rushing of munition supplies to the Mandated Islands is a significant sign.

Our Men Request: Our men requested not to give out a press release as I have done in the past without your consent. Kindly inform me of your decision. I honestly believe in informing the American public of what the Japanese militarists are doing against America—in the belief, once the Americans know these facts they will give full cooperation in the preparation for National Defense.

In the interest of America's security in the Pacific, I am

Very sincerely yours,
Kilsoo K. Haan

Note: Marshall Islands is the group of islands nearest to Hawaii—Pearl Harbor.

Haan's warnings were rebuffed in some cases and apparently ignored in others. One of the people honest enough to remember Haan's advance warning of the Pearl Harbor attack was Eric Sevareid, a newsman for CBS who had covered the fall of France to Nazi Germany in 1940. A man of immense integrity and also an anti-Nazi and ardent interventionist, Sevareid recalled many years later that Haan had offered detailed evidence to the State Department that Japan was planning a surprise attack and that Pearl Harbor would be the target. "One piece of evidence in the jigsaw was that a Korean working in the Japanese consulate in Honolulu had seen full blueprints of our above-water and underwater Naval installations—spread out on the consul's desk."

Sevareid recalled Haan's saying that he had been told by the White House press secretary, Stephen Early, that the State Department regarded the reports of the Sino-Korean People's League as the product of Haan's imagination, mere anti-Japanese propaganda. "He always ended up seeing very minor officials who took a very minor view of his warning," Sevareid remembered.

In October, Haan had urged a Japanese-American editor, Togo Tanaka, who had disputed his Korean underground reports to expose what Haan said was a Japanese consulate's attempt to conscript *Nisei*, Japanese born in the United States, to serve Japan. Haan had learned of this effort from several Japanese-Americans who were loyal to the United States and resented what they considered an attempt to coerce them into acting on Japan's behalf. Tanaka replied, "I have been told by the State Department that you are imagining the worst of Japan and the Japanese-American dual citizens. I am not aware of the conscription of Nisei, dual citizens by the Japanese Consulates. The so called Japan's war plan book and the surprise attack on Hawaii, in fact is the Japanese propaganda fiction to scare boys like you. So don't be alarmed and be afraid. The State Department considers you and your anti-Japan group 'troublemakers' and war mongers."

The next partisan to enter the controversy over Haan's credibility was Senator Gillette, a non-interventionist Democrat but a supporter of Korean independence and a friend of Haan's from as early as 1937. A veteran of the Spanish-American War and World War I, Gillette wrote to Colonel Rufus S. Bratton, the chief of the Far Eastern section of U.S. Army intelligence, asking if Tanaka was in fact employed as an advisor to Army intelligence. The report of Tanaka's relationship with Army intelligence, Bratton replied, "is false and without any foundation in fact."

There is no question that government officials received Haan's warnings. Some of them responded on official stationery.

April 26, 1941
My dear Mr. Haan:

Your letter of April 15, 1941 and its very interesting
enclosure are much appreciated. Some of your facts and
predictions have indeed been borne out by the passage
of time and I assure you that the information that you
have given us has always been highly appreciated.

Very sincerely yours,
Frank Knox
The Secretary of the Navy

During the first week of December, after five months of trying to
warn of a Pearl Harbor attack that he now believed would take
place in a matter of days, Haan made a final desperate attempt to
get the executive branch of the United States government to act
on his warnings. His last-minute information assault began with
an incident that could have been taken from an old Hollywood
movie.

"On the night of Dec. 3, 1941 I could not fall asleep," Haan
remembered a few weeks later.

I went to the Chinese Chop Suey House, the Chinese
Lantern, and ordered a bowl of Chinese soup called,
Won-ton. This was 11:45 pm when I got there.

Next to my table, a Japanese was trying to sell a
Chinese a second-hand automobile. After the Japanese
left, the Chinese said to me, "You like to buy cheap
automobile?" After a pause he said, "This Japanese is
selling four automobiles owned by the Japanese Embassy

workers because they are going to Japan pretty soon."
When I asked the Chinese what price he wants, he
replied, "oh so cheap."

The Japanese reportedly offered to sell a 1941 Buick
sedan for $1,000, a 1940 Buick coupe for $750, and a
1941 Buick coupe for $850.

Alarmed by what these Japanese bargains seemed to forebode and
agitated by his failure to be taken seriously by the State Department, Haan went home from the Chinese Lantern and wrote a
letter to Ambassador Nomura.

Dec. 3, 1941
Your Excellency:

I note that the embassy staff members are trying to sell
their automobiles. May I make the following offer:

Offer

I hereby submit $10.00 as an offer for the automobiles
you have for sale. I am sure this offer is a justified one
in the moral sense; since you have witnessed the International gangsterism in China and Korea which succeeded in looting millions of dollars worth of properties
from Koreans and the Chinese you would not miss it
very much if you would accept our offer. If and when
you do let me have them for $10.00 I would have them
auctioned for the benefit of the refugees, the victims of
Japanese aggression in China and Korea. At least, you
would be thankful that I would be in a position to do

this much for those helpless men and women and particularly the relatives of the Korean who threw the bomb
in Shanghai which resulted in the loss of your eye.

Very sincerely yours,
Kilsoo K. Haan

Nomura's response is not recorded, but like everyone else in
Washington, he had a lot to think about the next morning. On
December 4, 1941, the *Washington Times-Herald*, the largest
newspaper in the nation's capital, ran the headline "FDR'S WAR
PLANS!" The story was based on a copy of the Joint Planning
Board's "Rainbow 5," the blueprint for U.S. military operations
on multiple fronts in World War II, including the conscription of
ten million soldiers.

With Rainbow 5 now before the American public, Haan
made a last-ditch effort to warn the State Department that the
war would start at Pearl Harbor in the next few days. On December 5, he telephoned Maxwell Hamilton, the chief of the Division
of Far Eastern Affairs, informing him that Haan had been
warned by the Korean underground that the Japanese would
attack Pearl Harbor that weekend. Haan followed up with a
written memorandum:

Pursuant to our telephone conversations regarding our
agents' apprehensions that Japan may suddenly move
against Hawaii "this coming weekend," may I call
your attention to the following relevant and pertinent
information.

One: The publication of U.S. Army Air Corps maneuvers throughout the Hawaiian Islands by the Japanese
daily *Nippu Jiji*, Nov. 22, 1941. This timetable of air

maneuvers is from November through Dec. 31, 1941, "every day except Sundays and holidays." Two: The Italian magazine *Oggi* of Oct. 24, 1941, published an article in Rome forecasting war between Japan and America. The article forecast war between Japan and America by air and Naval attack of the Hawaiian Islands and eventually attacking Alaska, California and the Panama Canal.... It is our considered observation and sincere belief, December is the month of the Japanese attack and the SURPRISE FLEET is aimed at Hawaii, perhaps the first Sunday of December.... No matter how you feel toward our work, will you please convey our apprehension and this information to the President and to the military and Naval commanders in Hawaii.

Pearl Harbor was the worst day in the history of the U.S. Navy in terms of lives lost and ships damaged. The Japanese had lost twenty-nine airplanes and fifty-five flyers and all five two-man submarines. One submariner, Kazuo Sakamaki, passed out after he swam to the beach from his foundered sub and became the first Japanese POW of World War II. The national guardsman who captured him was a Japanese-American. The United States Army had gotten fourteen planes off the ground during the attack—there was no air cover when the Japanese arrived—and they accounted for ten of the downed Japanese fighters. One Japanese submarine used to launch the miniature submarines had disappeared, not in combat. Eighteen U.S. ships were sunk or damaged. Two thousand eight sailors and officers were killed, and 710 were wounded. One hundred nine Marines were killed and sixty-nine wounded. The Army lost 218 soldiers, with 364 wounded. Sixty-eight civilians were killed and thirty-five wounded, all but eight of them hit by stray shells from antiaircraft fire or by shells thrown off by

exploding ships. Only one Japanese bomb fell on the city of Honolulu, by mistake, but forty Navy and Army antiaircraft shells
destroyed or damaged homes, shops, and a school, doing half a
million dollars' worth of damage.

The collateral damage from U.S. fire did not fit well with how
Americans wanted to "remember Pearl Harbor." One case is
emblematic. Civilian workers at Pearl Harbor were ordered to
report for damage control work. Four riggers—Joseph Adams, his
son John Adams, Joe McCabe, a mixed-blood Irish-Hawaiian, and
McCabe's nephew, David Kahookele—were headed toward the
clouds of smoke when a misplaced Navy antiaircraft shell fell near
their vehicle. The car pivoted and stopped dead on four flat tires.
Joseph and Fata Kekahuna ran to help and found three of the men
dead and the fourth dying. A fragment from the same shell struck
twelve-year-old Matilda Faufata in the heart while she stood at her
front door watching. She died in a matter of moments. Everybody
in the neighborhood knew that the four riggers and the girl had
been killed by a stray U.S. shell, but for the next sixty years, photographs of the riddled car with two dead men visible in the front
seat would be displayed as "evidence" of Japanese strafing of civilians.

Misdirected U.S. antiaircraft shells also killed Patrick Chong,
the custodian of the local Carnegie library. Most of the civilian
victims were Japanese-American, Chinese-American, or Hawaiian.
Many were children. All were killed by stray American shells
except for three off-duty soldiers taking flying lessons, an airport
mechanic, a Japanese-American airport plumber who brought his
own gun to work in case of parachute troops, and four volunteer
firemen. But the myth that the Japanese had wantonly strafed
women and children—like the myth of treachery by American-born
Japanese—was frantically promoted by newspapers and Hollywood for decades afterward.

When the attack ended, half of the gun power of the Pacific Fleet was at the bottom of Pearl Harbor, and the United States had not a single functional battleship in the Pacific Ocean to face the Japanese Navy. Inexplicably, Admiral Chuichi Nagumo had failed to launch a third wave to destroy the oil tanks and dry docks that Dusko Popov had been sent to investigate. Most experts believe that if the oil tanks had exploded and torched the rest of the harbor, the United States would have lost Hawaii to Japan. For months afterward, U.S. currency issued to servicemen at Oahu was stamped "HAWAII" so the Japanese could not spend it elsewhere if they overwhelmed the garrison and seized the islands.

That afternoon, Kilsoo Haan, who had been unable to get through to most of the federal officials he tried to reach, even with the help of Senator Gillette, received a telephone call from Maxwell Hamilton. If his December 5 warning of an attack on Pearl Harbor were released to the press, Hamilton warned Haan, he would be "put away for the duration." On December 8, the FBI ordered him not to leave Washington, D.C., until further notice.

CHAPTER 11

THE SEARCH
FOR SCAPEGOATS

When the news about Pearl Harbor reached Washington, President Roosevelt was thunderstruck—not because he was surprised by the attack itself, but because the attack had been far more dreadful than anything the administration had expected. Secretary of Labor Frances Perkins, who saw him at a cabinet meeting that day, said that Roosevelt "could hardly bring himself to describe the devastation. His pride in the Navy was so terrific that he was having actual physical difficulty in getting out the words that put him on the record as knowing that the Navy was caught unawares." While Roosevelt himself had probably not actively conspired to provoke the Japanese, the Hull note had made war all but unavoidable, and he had done little to interfere.

Henry Stimson, the secretary of war, looking over the flurry of decoded documents, had known that war was about to break out. His concern was that the Japanese fire the first shot so Japan would be branded the aggressor by world opinion. And Harry Dexter White, of course, had intended to provoke the Japanese beyond any hope of peace.

The last tip-off had come in a decoded order from Tokyo to the Japanese consulate in Hawaii. The staff were ordered to break up their decoding machine and burn their files. Incredibly, nobody bothered to inform Admiral Kimmel and General Short of this virtual declaration that an attack was coming and Hawaii was the target. The information provided by Dusko Popov and Kilsoo Haan, that the target would be Pearl Harbor, was now confirmed by decoded messages from Japan's own diplomatic corps. Washington sat on the information—apparently because they wanted some sort of war but did not expect anything like what they got.

The last act of the tragedy was a farce. Intent on behaving in such a way as to make an early peace possible, the Japanese embassy had proposed to issue a formal declaration of war in Washington a half-hour before the actual attack on Pearl Harbor. The declaration had been postponed until the last few hours in the vain hope that something would head off a catastrophic war. Mitsuo Fuchida, the Japanese flight commander, had strict orders not to drop the first bombs before eight o'clock a.m., as he revealed in a confidential memoir hidden in a safe in his son's New Jersey home until everyone concerned had died. Tokyo sent a fourteen-part encoded message to its embassy in Washington informing its diplomats that the decision for war had been made. American decoders were on duty all night, so the White House knew about the message before the embassy did. As he read the thirteenth part of the decoded message, Roosevelt turned to his alter ego, Harry Hopkins—a communist sympathizer according to "Bill"

Akhmerov—and said bluntly, "This means war." This was at nine o'clock in the evening of December 6—ample time to get a warning to Kimmel and Short at Pearl Harbor—but nobody telephoned Hawaii from the White House. When the final part of the war message arrived at the Japanese embassy, the typists had all gone home and the diplomats themselves—horrified by the prospect of war—had gotten so drunk the night before that they could not get the declaration of war typed in time. Kurusu and Nomura dropped it off as the planes were returning to their carriers from the smoking wreckage of the Pacific Fleet.

The Japanese message read in part, "It is a fact of history that the countries of East Asia for the past hundred years or more have been compelled to observe the status quo under the Anglo-American policy of imperialistic exploitation and to sacrifice themselves to the prosperity of the two nations." Cordell Hull was not ready for that kind of talk from "colored people." "In all my fifty years of public service I have never seen a document that was more crowded with infamous falsehoods and distortions—infamous falsehoods and distortions on a scale so huge that I never imagined until today that any government on this planet was capable of uttering them," Hull said tersely. Privately, Hull referred to Kurusu and Nomura as "scoundrels and piss-ants." Franklin Roosevelt's own family, however, lent at least some credibility to the historical allegations in the Japanese declaration of war, for the Delanos had made a huge fortune in the Chinese opium trade. However much Hirohito's government had made Showa Japan hated throughout Asia, the declaration accurately depicted the history of Western relations with the East as all Asians understood it.

General Marshall had supposedly been out riding his horse when the decoded messages reached his office—though some observers said he was actually in the building when the message came in. The Army sent a telegram rather than use the telephone.

A Japanese-American Western Union boy on a motorcycle delivered it while the attack was already in progress. Marshall responded to the debacle of the attack with one of the strangest statements ever attributed to him: "Pearl Harbor was the only installation we had anywhere that was reasonably well equipped. Therefore we were not worried about it. In our opinion the commanders had been alerted. In our opinion there was nothing more we could give them.... In our opinion it was the one place that had enough within itself to put up a reasonable defense. The only place we had any assurance about was Hawaii." And indeed, with two battleships sunk and the other six disabled and almost three hundred aircraft destroyed or damaged, it was now impossible to reinforce the Philippines, where twenty thousand American troops, many of them peacetime draftees, were stuck in Japan's back yard with outmoded equipment.

The garrison there heard about Pearl Harbor while the attack was still in progress and had gone on the alert. It was there at 12:45 p.m. the following day, as thousands of red-blooded Americans rushed to volunteer and avenge the "sneak attack," that the second act of the tragedy took place. The United States had hoped to have at least one hundred B-17s in the Philippines before war broke out. So far they had received thirty-five. These were the long-range four-engine bombers that Admiral Kimmel had wanted for armed reconnaissance around Hawaii but never got. The U.S. decided to attack the Japanese on Formosa, and the B-17s were called down to Clark Field to refuel and arm. While their pilots and gunners were lunching and the planes were refueling, a formation of two-engine Japanese bombers arrived and carried out a precision bombing run from twenty thousand feet. Clark Field exploded in flame and smoke, and eighteen of the twenty-one B-17s on the field were destroyed in a matter of minutes. Japanese Mitsubishi A6M Zero fighters zoomed in to strafe the P-40 and P-36 fighters at Eba and Nichols Fields. In addition to the B-17s at Clark, the Japanese destroyed fifty-three of the 107 U.S. fighters in the Philippines and thirty-five other supply and training aircraft, losing only seven of their own fighters. Not a single U.S. fighter plane had been aloft to oppose them, and many of the surviving fighters were obsolete P-36 Seversky ships, second-string aircraft that stood no chance against a Zero in a dogfight. Most of the P-36 fighters were destroyed in the next few days, and the fleet of P-40s—obsolescent if not obsolete—was whittled down until there were two left. The American infantrymen who called themselves "the Battling Bastards of Bataan—no Mama, no Papa, no Uncle Sam" referred to their two-plane air cover as the Lone Ranger and Tonto. When the Battling Bastards who survived the battle and the Bataan Death March were dying in Japanese prison camps of *sekiri*—tropical diarrhea with bloody stools—they wrote curses on the prison walls in their own fecal blood: "____ Roosevelt," "____ MacArthur," "____ the Japs." As in his presidential campaigns, FDR came in first.

Pearl Harbor also spelled the doom of the U.S. Asiatic Fleet, which had patrolled the coast of China from its base in the Philippines. Unable to survive Japanese air attacks without American air cover, the Asiatic Fleet joined the Dutch, British, and Australian warships trying to stop the Japanese from seizing the Dutch East Indies and obtaining the oil they needed. In a series of battles culminating on February 27, 1942, the Allied fleet clashed with a Japanese fleet of roughly the same size. It was a sea-going massacre. The Japanese sank the cruiser USS *Houston* and two American destroyers, along with most of the Dutch, British, and Australian ships for a combined Allied loss of ten ships and 2,173 officers and sailors—almost as many dead as at Pearl Harbor. A U.S. destroyer that escaped the battle, the *Edsall*, disappeared with all 153 hands.

For good measure, Japanese Naval aircraft sank the venerable USS *Langley*, the Navy's first aircraft carrier, while she was transporting aircraft to defend the Dutch East Indies. Allied morale plummeted as defeat after defeat convinced disheartened white soldiers that the Japanese were not monkeys but supermen. Faced with losses and humiliations they had not anticipated when they dictated unacceptable conditions to a proud but threatened nation—now enraged and filled with ferocious self-confidence—Roosevelt and the men around him began a frantic search for scapegoats.

Their first target was Admiral Husband Kimmel. As his predecessor Richardson had done, Kimmel had warned the president about the Navy's lack of preparation for war. Roosevelt, however, did not warn Kimmel about the impending attack on Pearl Harbor—not even after he had read the decoded Japanese message on December 6. Ten days after the attack, Kimmel and General Walter Short were both demoted and replaced.

Kimmel saw it coming. As he watched the last phase of the attack on the morning of December 7, a spent .50-caliber slug from one of his fleet's own antiaircraft machine guns hit Kimmel in the chest, shredded his white linen uniform, and tumbled to the ground at his feet. Kimmel stooped over, picked up the half-inch-wide bullet, and looked at it glumly: "It would have been merciful had it killed me."

General Short took his demotion humbly. Kimmel—whom Roosevelt had appointed because he was a scrapper—fought for the rest of his life to win exoneration. "The Pacific Fleet deserved a fighting chance," Kimmel wrote in *Admiral Kimmel's Story*, published in 1954. "Had we had as much as two hours of warning a full alert of planes and guns would have greatly reduced the damage. We could possibly have been able to locate the Jap carriers, and our own carriers *Lexington* and *Enterprise* already at sea to the westward of Oahu might have been brought into the picture instead of expending their efforts to the southward as a result of faulty information. The great intangible, the element of surprise, would have been denied the Japs."

Some people assert that Kimmel was not entirely blameless. An hour before the bombs began to fall, the crew of USS *Antares*, a World War I–vintage transport pulling a barge, spotted a Japanese two-man submarine trying to shadow the *Antares* into Pearl Harbor. The *Antares* put out a warning, a twin-engine Catalina dropped smoke pots, and the USS *Ward*, a destroyer patrolling the harbor entrance, opened fire and hit the conning tower twice with her four-inch gun. The *Ward*'s depth charges then lifted the submarine visibly out of the water and the sub sank.

The *Ward* and the *Antares* both radioed news of the attack. The reports were shrugged off ashore, even though newspapers all over the United States had been predicting war with Japan for days, and that morning's *Honolulu Advertiser* carried the eight-column banner headline "F.D.R. WILL SEND MESSAGE TO EMPEROR ON WAR CRISIS." The question whether Kimmel was substantially to blame for a lack of vigilance remains open. But why didn't the White House or the War Department telephone Hawaii when the president read the decoded message and said, "This means war"? That question is unanswered by anything Kimmel did or did not do.

Pearl Harbor had been an obvious target—so obvious, in fact, that John Huston was at work at the time on a movie about a fictional Japanese air attack on Pearl Harbor. After the attack, Huston scurried to change the target in the film from Pearl Harbor to the Panama Canal. The film kept its original title, *Across the Pacific*, perhaps because it was almost completed when the Japanese struck. Had the film been released before the attack, Roosevelt's embarrassment might have been even deeper than it was.

In an audience with Hirohito on December 26, Mitsuo Fuchida, Admiral Nagumo, Captain Osami Nagano, and the leader of the second wave of attackers at Pearl Harbor, Shigekazu Shimazaki, presented the emperor with photographs of the cataclysmic destruction of the Pacific Fleet. The audience was supposed to last for thirty minutes, but Hirohito was so fascinated by the photographs that he extended it to almost two hours.

"Are there any other questions, Your Majesty?" Nagano asked.

"Not particularly..." the emperor replied. Then, after a few moments, he asked: "Are you going to take these pictures with you when you go?"

"We'll put a cover on it and present it to Your Majesty later," Nagano said.

"Oh, you could put the cover on later," Hirohito replied. "I'd like to show this to the empress now." The emperor shuffled away clutching ten photographs, and the warriors bowed obediently. Hirohito knew that the attack had saved his throne and his dynasty from revolution, at least for the time being, and he may have hoped that the catastrophes of Pearl Harbor and Clark Field had convinced the Americans to be reasonable. A pilot who had strafed Officer's Row hoping to kill a few admirals had been harshly rebuked when he reported back to his carrier. The Japanese wanted the attack to be conducted with chivalry, as in the hostilities with Russia in 1904 and with the Kaiser's forces in 1914, so they could negotiate a peace as honorable men and not as the rapists of Nanking.

Three days after the attack on Pearl Harbor, Henry Morgenthau Jr. asked J. Edgar Hoover what he thought about rounding up the entire Japanese and Japanese-American population of the west coast. Hoover was appalled and bluntly told Morgenthau that Attorney General Francis Biddle would not approve any "dragnet or round-up procedure." Many of these ethnic Japanese were American citizens, Hoover reminded Morgenthau, and such an action would be illegal. He also knew that such a move was unnecessary. Based on information from loyal Japanese-Americans, including Togo Tanaka, and from Korean dissidents, including Kilsoo Haan, as well as information obtained by burglarizing the Japanese consulate in Los Angeles and the Black Dragon Society's office, Hoover had a comprehensive list of people he wanted to arrest, and he had already started.

"We think the Japanese Government is stupid and has embarked on a campaign it has absolutely no chance of winning," Togo Tanaka had written in a newspaper editorial published on December 8. The Japanese-American community "had not been in sympathy with Japan's expansion program," he insisted. Tanaka was arrested the same day, with no explanation, and was in custody as Hoover spoke to Morgenthau and opposed a wholesale round-up. Tanaka was held for eleven days and then released without formal charges or an explanation. Officials from the War Department—more political than the FBI and less informed about legality—had interrogated Tanaka about his loyalties earlier when he had asked if his bilingual newspaper could keep publishing in case of war with Japan.

Tanaka estimated that about 5 percent of the Japanese-born population might be suspect. He divided the suspects about evenly into *aka*, "reds," who tended to be educated but unsuccessful, and ultra-nationalists, who tended to be thick-headed and unable to learn English. Within three weeks of the attack on Pearl Harbor, the FBI, the Bureau of Naval intelligence, and the Bureau of Army Intelligence had arrested 2,192 Japanese within the continental United States and another 879 in Hawaii. Some of these people were actually dangerous—even under detention, Japanese fanatics murdered a couple Japanese-Americans for their loyalty to the United States—but many others were simply victims of circumstance.

The FBI and Naval intelligence were satisfied now that Tanaka's potentially dangerous 5 percent were in custody, but the Roosevelt administration—especially Morgenthau—was definitely not satisfied. The men who were responsible for the disaster at Pearl Harbor, through incompetence if not treason, promoted a narrative of inexplicable and unprovoked Japanese aggression. With the cooperation of the press and eventually Hollywood, the administration depicted Pearl Harbor as an unforeseen attack on a friendly nation and Japan as an implacable war machine intent on joining Hitler in global conquest. In a cartoon titled "Waiting for the Signal from Home," Theodore Geisel—"Dr. Seuss"—depicted a multitude of buck-toothed Japanese queuing up from Washington State to California in an "Honorable 5th Column" to receive their saboteurs' bundles of TNT. Under protest, J. Edgar Hoover sent the FBI to break into selected Japanese-American homes to confiscate weapons, cameras, and radios needed for an imagined uprising. Kilsoo Haan, projecting his hatred of Japanese militarists onto Japanese-Americans, joined racist Americans in urging that the whole population be "evacuated" from the west coast.

On March 18, 1942, Roosevelt signed Executive Order 9102, establishing the War Relocation Authority, which Senator Robert Taft called the sloppiest criminal law he had ever heard of. Japanese-Americans born and raised in the United States, many of them Christians, many of them graduates of American high schools and colleges, were moved on a few days' notice to ten concentration camps in isolated mountain and desert locations. Some collapsed of heat stroke before they arrived at the hastily constructed tar-paper and clapboard barracks, where multiple families shared a single room. By June 7, 112,000 American men, women, and children were interned behind barbed wire, eating wretched food in harsh climates. About a dozen inmates were shot dead by guards, and many others were beaten, sometimes to avenge a fallen brother or friend, sometimes because they wandered outside the safety zone, often trying to catch fish to supplement their rations. Many elderly Japanese succumbed to culture shock and simply gave up the will to live. Eleanor Roosevelt spoke out against the internments—the relocated Japanese artist Chiura Obata sent her one of his paintings as a sign of gratitude—and Attorney General Biddle moved behind the scenes to liberalize a release program for Japanese-Americans who could prove their loyalty. The Communist Party USA, on the other hand, strongly supported relocation "for the good of the war effort," and the American Civil Liberties Union generally acquiesced for the good of the Roosevelt administration. The average Japanese-American from California, Oregon, or Washington spent about nine hundred days in concentration camps during World War II for a single crime—the wrong racial background.

On December 11, 1941, four days after Pearl Harbor, Hitler spontaneously declared war on the United States. With the Wehrmacht at the gates of Moscow and Leningrad, Russian morale was crumbling. NKVD detachments were being placed behind Red Army positions to shoot deserters. Then hundreds of thousands of reinforcements and more than a thousand tanks arrived from Siberia and Mongolia, freed up by the Japanese war with the United States. Snow fell at the same time, and the Russians stopped the Wehrmacht in its tracks, saved Moscow and Leningrad, and drove the Germans into a limited retreat.

Vitalii Pavlov's lunch date with Harry Dexter White at the Old Ebbitt Grill might have been the Soviets' most important strategic maneuver.

On January 20, 1942, SS-Obergruppenführer Reinhard Heydrich convened a conference at Wannsee, a suburb of Berlin, to plot the fate of Europe's Jews. Heydrich must have known, though he did not mention it, that with both Russia and America in the war and with the German invasion of Russia repulsed, Germany faced a long and perhaps unwinnable war. The large-scale relocation of the millions of Jews now under the control of the Third Reich was no longer practicable, and Heydrich presented a program of extermination.

> Under proper guidance, in the course of the final solution the Jews are to be allocated for appropriate labor in the East. Able-bodied Jews, separated according to sex, will be taken in large work columns to these areas for work on roads, in the course of which action doubtless a large portion will be eliminated by natural causes. The possible final remnant will, since it will undoubtedly consist of the most resistant portion, have to be treated accordingly, because it is the product of natural selection and would, if released, act as the seed of a new Jewish revival. See the experience of history.

Thus with a nod to Darwin, Heydrich signed the death warrant of the Jews as a race. He exempted those over sixty-five because they were unlikely to breed and those who had been crippled or decorated in World War I for patriotic reasons. Everyone else was to be murdered. Pearl Harbor had saved Stalin. But the entry of America into the war, with the maniacal cooperation of Hitler, had touched off the Final Solution.

CHAPTER 12

NEMESIS

Harry Dexter White changed history by engineering the diplomatic responses that led to the attack on Pearl Harbor and stranding, consequently, thirty thousand Americans in the Philippines to be decimated by the vengeful Japanese. Toward the end of the war, hundreds of thousands of Japanese civilians would die by incendiary bombs and nuclear attack. And millions of Koreans would perish in World War II's aftershock on the Korean peninsula. But Stalin was saved from his treacherous one-time ally, Hitler, and the Russian and eastern European peoples, along with the East Germans, would endure four more decades of post-Stalinist oppression. As for White himself, the Soviets quietly arranged to pay for his daughters' college tuition.

White's other contributions to the reconstruction of the postwar world were less obviously treasonous but often mischievous. A week after Pearl Harbor, White was put in charge of financial aid to Nationalist China. Chiang Kai-shek's regime probably would have collapsed without any help from Harry Dexter White—Chiang's reluctance to pay or to lead his own troops was notorious—but at the height of Chiang's troubles, White cut off his credit, contributing to the communist victory in China that both the Japanese and the Americans had dreaded and hoped to prevent.

White represented the United States in the 1944 Bretton Woods Conference, which established a new international financial and monetary system. At the end of the conference, control of the global economy had been wrested away from Great Britain and dropped in the lap of the United States—perhaps temporarily, as far as White was concerned.

After the war, White handed over the printing plates for occupation currency to the Soviets so they could print money to be spent in postwar occupied Germany, undercutting the purchasing power of U.S. troops to be stationed there, and further disrupting the German economy.

White—along with his boss, Henry Morgenthau—finally overreached himself in September 1944 at the Second Quebec Conference, where Roosevelt, Churchill, and Canadian Prime Minister Mackenzie King met to discuss the postwar fate of Germany. Here Roosevelt proposed the so-called Morgenthau Plan—almost certainly drafted by White—which would have de-industrialized Germany and divided the country into five separate agricultural states with no heavy industry whatsoever. FDR pushed the plan on a reluctant Churchill, who initially called it "un-Christian-like," with a bribe of $6 billion from American taxpayers to rebuild Britain after the war.

Secretary of War Henry Stimson, who was already planning the reconstruction of Europe with a view to containing Stalin, was appalled to find that Morgenthau and White had virtually taken control of the Roosevelt administration. "It is a terrible thing to think that the total power of the United States and the United Kingdom in such a critical matter as this is in the hands of two men, both of whom are similar in their impulsiveness and their lack of systematic study," Stimson wrote in his diary for September 16–17. "I have yet to meet a man who is not horrified with the 'Carthaginian' attitude of the Treasury. It is Semitism gone wild for vengeance and, if ultimately carried out (I can't believe that it will be) it sure as fate will lay the seeds for another war in the next generation. And yet these two men in a brief conference in Quebec with nobody to advise them except 'yes-men', with no Cabinet minister with the President except Morgenthau, have taken this step and given directions for it to be carried out."

Stimson hated White's idea, though he did not realize that the real motive behind the Morgenthau Plan was far more sinister than simple revenge for Nazi brutality. Stimson understood that without a unified Germany's industrial and military strength, there was nothing between the Red Army and the English Channel but the war-weary countries that had been overwhelmed in 1940 by Hitler's second-string tanks, bolt-action rifles, and horse-drawn supply wagons. Without a strong Germany, Western Europe was indefensible. Harry Dexter White, Stalin's man in Washington, was going to make sure that there was no strong Germany, or any Germany at all that was not under Stalin's control.

Even though the Morgenthau Plan was never implemented, it nevertheless harmed the West, and it did so in a way that White probably did not foresee. After the Allied landings in Normandy on June 6, 1944, many German troops, seeing that defeat was inevitable, developed an unspoken strategy—fight on fiercely against the Russians in the east and gradually collapse in the west, where the British, the French, and the Americans could be expected to settle for a traditional and humane peace with Germany once Hitler and his thugs had been executed. The bomb plot of July 20, in which Hitler was wounded, was part of a German plan to form a new government to negotiate with the Western Allies. Once Hitler recovered and executed his would-be assassins, this silent strategy plan was thwarted. When Nazi propagandists made America's plans for postwar Germany widely known, Germans realized that the very survival of their country and society was at stake. The Morgenthau Plan stiffened German resistance despite exhaustion and hopelessness. The Republican presidential nominee, Thomas Dewey, said the Morgenthau Plan was worth ten divisions to Hitler.

The ultimate German response to the Morgenthau Plan was the Battle of the Bulge, the bloodiest contest of the war for the U.S., with 19,246 dead, 62,489 men wounded or crippled by frostbite, and 26,612 captured or missing. The Germans' ferocious offensive cost them the chance to let the American, British, and French forces take all or most of Germany and forestall a vengeful Soviet invasion. Pearl Harbor was Harry Dexter White's first military victory for Stalin. The Battle of the Bulge was his last.

Finland was a reluctant ally of Nazi Germany, a country the Finns disliked, against Stalin, a dictator they detested. The Finns had no animus against the United States. In 1944, the Finns sold a partially burned Soviet code-book picked up on a battlefield to "Wild Bill" Donovan of the OSS, predecessor of the CIA, for $15,000. This windfall, and the decoding work of a mathematical genius named Meredith Gardner and his colleagues, enabled the U.S. Army Signal Intelligence Service to read the encoded messages that the NKVD had been sending to their agents in the United States since the 1930s.

The Signal Intelligence Service had saved these intercepted but inscrutable NKVD messages, and when they began to read them, a Soviet agent usually code-named "Jurist" turned up. The Soviets never identified Jurist by name, but once the intelligence team began to read the NKVD codes, it followed Jurist's exploits closely and discovered that he was very close to Henry Morgenthau. The messages indicated that Jurist and Morgenthau traveled to London and Normandy as a two-man team, leaving the United States on August 5, 1944. Intelligence operatives checked to see who had traveled with Morgenthau on specific dates to specific destinations. The pieces of the puzzle formed a coherent picture—the Soviet agent known as Jurist was Harry Dexter White.

The decoding operation, known as VENONA, was so secret that even President Roosevelt and Vice President Harry S. Truman did not know about it. When Eleanor Roosevelt somehow learned that the U.S. Army was reading Stalin's spy messages, she was horrified at the betrayal of trust and ordered the Army to stop. The Signal Intelligence Service shrugged her off, but—apparently through trusted friends of Mrs. Roosevelt—the Soviets got wind of VENONA and infiltrated the project. The Soviets changed their code books—the American code-breakers were ordered to return their half-burned copy—and the work of VENONA, still top secret, came to an end. But Harry Dexter White was now on the books as a Soviet agent.

The ground under White's feet had been somewhat shaky even before he was identified as VENONA's "Jurist." Whittaker Chambers had not mentioned White in his first denunciation of Soviet agents, but on September 2, 1939, the day after Hitler invaded Poland, a Jewish anti-communist reporter, Isaac Don

Levine, arranged a meeting between Chambers and Assistant Secretary of State Adolf Berle, the State Department's internal security director. Berle, though not a communist, was a man of the left, and his notes make no mention of White. But Levine claimed afterward that Chambers had mentioned White by name. Berle passed a four-page list of the Soviet agents and intense sympathizers whom Chambers had identified in Levine's presence on to Roosevelt, who dismissed the accusation as "absurd." Unofficial sources indicate that the president used a more scatological term. J. Edgar Hoover supposedly agreed with Roosevelt, or pretended to in order to hang onto his job. This left White safe to conspire with Vitalii Pavlov in 1941.

On March 20, 1945—the Army was now decoding the VENONA papers—State Department security officer Raymond Murphy called Chambers in again. Murphy's notes state that Chambers identified Harry Dexter White as a rather timid member at large of Soviet intelligence. Chambers also stated that White had brought a number of American communists into the Treasury Department under his own protection.

On April 12, 1945, Franklin Delano Roosevelt died of a stroke while having his portrait painted. Loyal to the last to people who had been loyal to him—and remarkably vindictive to anyone who opposed him—FDR had unwittingly given cover to Harry Dexter White and other suspected communists in the State and Treasury Departments, refusing to question their private or secret politics as long as they flattered him and deferred to him.

Henry Morgenthau knew that the new president, Harry Truman, did not like him, and in May he stepped down as secretary of the Treasury. White had lost his patron. He was finished—but he was in denial about it.

Just how much hubris White had developed serving as the economic brains behind Morgenthau and Roosevelt became apparent in August 1945 when he got into a confrontation with a Jonathan Mitchell, who had written speeches for Morgenthau. As Mitchell later told a Senate subcommittee, he had been interviewing White over lunch when White mentioned Harold Laski, a Marxist and anti-Christian professor at the London School of Economics whom White greatly admired.

"He asked me if I didn't think he was a great man, and in particular what I thought of his latest book." Mitchell explained that the thesis of Laski's book, *Faith, Reason, and Civilization*, was that private business or capitalism had proved itself inadequate, that the Christian faith no longer had any validity, and that, happily, the Russians had worked out a new system of economics and a new faith that would replace capitalism and Christianity.

> I didn't wish to be controversial about anything, and I said what I thought was the universal opinion about Mr. Laski, that he was a charming teller of cockney stories, but intellectually a lightweight. This infuriated Mr. White. He then read me a very long lecture.... Mr. White said that this was by all odds the most profound book which had been written in our lifetime and that no one had foreseen with such uncanny accuracy and depth the way in which the world was going.... So far as I remember, he at no occasion used the word "communism". He expressed extravagant approval of Mr. Laski's book, which was a eulogy of communism.... I expressed mild dissent at Mr. White's argument, and at each dissent he became more and more upset, and toward the end of the lunch, he arose and

advanced upon me with his arms swinging.... Mr. [Herbert] Gaston arose and put his arms around Mr. White and they waltzed back and forth for three to four minutes until Mr. White became calmer and agreed to sit down. That more or less destroyed the spirit of the lunch... he was extremely angry... he was in a towering rage.

White had stepped out of character in openly advocating the Russian system, otherwise known as communism, to Mitchell, whom he may have assumed was a fellow traveler until Mitchell dismissed Laski as a "lightweight." He consistently told his Soviet contacts that he would gladly die for the Revolution but that his exposure would cause a scandal that could damage the cause. Herbert Gaston, another Treasury official, also seemed to have been surprised by White's vehemence. Even without Roosevelt and Morgenthau to cover for him, White obviously felt self-confident enough to drop his pose as a conservative economist and tacitly admit he was a communist sympathizer—though not a Soviet agent. That disclosure came next.

Elizabeth Bentley, who as a confused graduate student in Italy first applauded and then rejected Mussolini's fascism, later became the lover of Jacob Golos, a Soviet spymaster who used her as a courier through the late 1930s and early 1940s, much as Whittaker Chambers had served as a courier until he dropped out in 1938. After Golos died in her arms in 1943, Bentley was transferred to a new handler, the deplorable Boris Bykov, whom she did not like, much less love, and she defected. On November 7, 1945, Bentley told the FBI that one of the Soviets' sources of information was Harry Dexter White. The next day, J. Edgar Hoover sent a letter to Truman's military aide, General Harry Vaughn, listing a dozen Soviet sources Bentley had identified. Harry Dexter White was the second name on the list.

On December 4, 1945, the FBI—which was allowed access to the still-secret VENONA decrypts—followed up with a more detailed letter sent to the White House, the attorney general, and the State Department, again naming White. Six weeks later, Truman nevertheless nominated White to be the director of the International Monetary Fund. The FBI sent the White House a twenty-four-page memorandum detailing White's Soviet contacts, yet the nomination went through. A man identified as a Soviet agent had been put in charge of one of the most important economic institutions of the free world.

White was the director of the International Monetary Fund until his abrupt resignation on June 17, 1947. He reportedly cleaned out his records and took them away in a truck without even saying good-bye. Truman later said that as soon as he learned of White's Soviet connections, he terminated him from the Treasury and the IMF. But the lag between February 1946 and June 1947 remained unexplained. White was now done with the government. But the government was not done with White.

On July 31, 1948, Elizabeth Bentley appeared before the House Un-American Activities Committee (HUAC). The committee had investigated Nazi influence and was now investigating Soviet espionage activities in the United States. Bentley identified White as a member of the Silvermaster group, a ring of communist agents organized by Nathan Gregory Silvermaster, an economist at the War Production Board. Members of the group worked for the U.S. government and transferred information to the Soviets. "Harry Dexter White... I believe he was Assistant Secretary of the Treasury and head of Monetary Research as I recall.... I don't know whether Mr. White was a card-carrying Communist or not... he gave information to Mr. Silvermaster which was relayed to me."

Three days later the committee heard from Whittaker Chambers: "I can't positively say that he is a registered member of the

Communist Party but he certainly was a fellow traveler so far within the fold that his not being a Communist would be a mistake on both sides.... I didn't ask him to leave the Communist Party, but to break away from the Communist movement.... He left me in a very agitated frame of mind, and I thought I had succeeded. Apparently I did not."

Chambers tried to explain that White, an agent of influence, was more important than an ordinary spy because he could shape policy instead of just revealing secrets. "I should perhaps make the point that these people were specifically not wanted to act as sources of information," Chambers told HUAC. "These people were an elite group, an outstanding group, which it was believed would rise to positions—as indeed some of them did—notably Mr. White, Mr. [Alger] Hiss—in the Government, and their positions in the Government would be of very much more service to the Communist Party."

White asked for an opportunity to appear before the committee to clear his name. He probably did not know that the Signal Intelligence Service and the FBI knew that he was "Jurist." He did know, however, that Chambers and Bentley were both admitted communist agents with records of disloyalty, drinking problems, and unsavory sex lives. Harry Dexter White was a model of normality—World War I veteran; an academic with degrees from Columbia, Harvard, and Stanford; very moderate drinker; good father; and faithful husband of a gifted wife who was a popular children's author. He also knew that he might have been the most intelligent man in the Roosevelt administration, far more intelligent than Henry Morgenthau Jr., Cordell Hull, or Roosevelt himself. He may have hoped that he could simply steamroll a couple of profligate drunkards like Whittaker Chambers and

Elizabeth Bentley. The only problem was that Chambers and Bentley, for all their flaws, were telling the truth.

The members of the House Un-American Activities Committee were unlikely to intimidate a man of White's intellect and experience. The chairman, J. Parnell Thomas, was under indictment for a kick-back scheme. (He was later convicted and served nine months of a two-year sentence.) John Rankin of Mississippi was a hard-core racist who summed up his support for Japanese-American relocation with memorable logic—"A Jap is a Jap." He also regarded almost all Jews as communists who used their influence to stir up blacks. The other members were less colorful. Karl Mundt, an anti-communist Republican from South Dakota and future senator, held degrees from Carleton College in Minnesota and Columbia University, but he had spent his life as a high school speech and history teacher until he discovered politics. John McDowell, from Pennsylvania, was no threat either—a graduate of Randolph-Macon Military Academy who lost more elections than he won. Then there was the young fellow from California with the jowls and the five-o'clock shadow, Richard Nixon. Whittier College? Where was that? The chief investigator was Robert E. Stripling. Roosevelt had tried to get the committee abolished not once but twice, because the previous chairman, Martin Dies, a six-foot-four blond Texan, spent most of his time investigating communists instead of the German American Bund and other home-grown fascists. With J. Parnell Thomas as the chairman, the proceeding would probably be a big joke. Thomas was bald, stubby, and pink, with a child's features, and when he was contradicted he would bounce in his seat, slamming the table with his fists. Harry Dexter White knew he was smarter than any of them, maybe smarter than all of them put together.

White got the hearing he had requested on August 13, 1948. The Marshall Plan to rebuild Europe, including Germany, had replaced the Morgenthau Plan the year before. Jan Masaryk, the leader of democracy in Czechoslovakia, had been found dead in a courtyard after a fall from a window in March 1948—arguments raged over whether the death was suicide or murder. The Chinese communists had been giving Chiang Kai-shek a very bad time once the Japanese had left China. When the Russians blockaded Berlin in June, the Americans and British responded with the Berlin Airlift. American and British pilots risked their necks flying food and coal into Berlin. War with Stalin's Russia seemed a real possibility. The Berlin Airlift was in its second month when Harry Dexter White spoke.

After White recounted his educational and professional background for the committee, Stripling asked him if he was acquainted with Nathan Gregory Silvermaster. "I know Mr. Silvermaster pretty well," White acknowledged. The drama that ensued comes through vividly in the transcript of the hearing. White asked for permission to read a prepared statement of his personal "creed."

> WHITE: I voluntarily asked to come here before this committee, and the committee has been kind to grant my request. I have read in the newspaper charges that have been made against me by a Miss Elizabeth Bentley, and a Mr. Whittaker Chambers. I am coming before you because I think it is important that the truth be made known to the committee, and to the public, and I am prepared to answer to the best of my ability any questions that any member of the committee may wish to ask.

I should like to state at the start that I am not now and never have been a Communist, nor even close to becoming one; that I cannot recollect ever knowing either a Miss Bentley or a Mr. Whittaker Chambers, nor, judging from the pictures I have seen in the press, have I ever met them.

The press reported that the witnesses claim that I helped to obtain key posts for persons I know were engaged in espionage work to help them in the work. That allegation is unqualifiedly false.

There is and can be no basis in fact whatever for such a charge.

The principles in which I believe, and by which I live, make it impossible for me to ever do a disloyal act or anything against the interests of our country, and I have jotted down what my belief is for the committee's information.

My creed is the American creed. I believe in freedom of religion, freedom of speech, freedom of thought, freedom of the press, freedom of criticism, and freedom of movement. I believe in the goal of equality of opportunity, and the right of each individual to follow the calling of his or her own choice, and the right of every individual to an opportunity to develop his or her capacity to the fullest.

I believe in the right and duty of every citizen to work for, to expect, and to obtain an increasing measure of political, economic, and emotional security for all. I am opposed to discrimination in any form, whether on grounds of race, color, religion, political belief, or economic status.

I believe in the freedom of choice of one's representatives in Government, untrammeled by machine guns, secret police, or a police state.

I am opposed to arbitrary and unwarranted use of power or authority from whatever source or against any individual or group.

I believe in a government of law, not of men, where law is above any man, and not any man above law.

I consider these principles sacred. I regard them as the basic fabric of our American way of life, and I believe in them as living realities, and not as my words on paper.

That is my creed. Those are the principles I have worked for. Together those are the principles that I have been prepared in the past to fight for, and am prepared to defend at any time with my life, if need be.

That is all I am going to say at this time. I am ready for any questions you may wish to ask. [Applause.]

Stripling continued by asking White if he was acquainted with various members of the Silvermaster group. After White acknowledged knowing all but one of them, Stripling took up his acquaintance with Whittaker Chambers.

STRIPLING: Did you ever know anyone in 1935 or 1936 who went under the name of Carl, C-a-r-l?

WHITE: I do not recollect any such name. I may have; it is a long time ago.

STRIPLING: Did you ever know—I believe you stated you did not know a person by the name of Whittaker Chambers?

WHITE: To the best of my recollection I remember no such name.

STRIPLING: Now, Mr. Chambers has testified that he was the courier for a Communist apparatus, operating in the Government in 1935, and 1936, and part of 1937. He testified that he was known only as Carl to the members of that apparatus. And I ask you again, do you remember any person in that period known to you only as Carl?

WHITE: I have no recollection. I doubt very much whether I would have known any man by just the first name. It would have been very peculiar.

Stripling then returned to White's connection to the Silvermaster group.

STRIPLNG: How many times would you say you had been at the home of Nathan Gregory Silvermaster?

WHITE: Oh, over the years, I suppose, half a dozen times, maybe a little more, maybe a little less.

STRIPLING: Did you ever go into Mr. Silvermaster's basement at 5515 30th Street?

WHITE: Yes, they asked me that question before, and I listened to the question being asked of Mr. [Lauchlin] Currie [Roosevelt's economic advisor and a member of the Silvermaster group].

THE CHAIRMAN: Whom do you mean by "they"?

WHITE: Did somebody ask me something?

THE CHAIRMAN: Whom do you mean by "they" asked you the question before?

WHITE: At the grand jury. Maybe I am anticipating, so I will pass that. I was collecting my memory. Yes, I was at the basement. It was at a party, and they were playing ping-pong. I fancied myself a little as a ping-pong player, and we played a few times.

THE CHAIRMAN: Just a minute, right there. Let me see that note. One thing I cannot reconcile, Mr. White, you send me a note and you say that:

I am recovering from a severe heart attack. I would appreciate it if the chairman would give me five or ten minutes rest after each hour.

For a person who had a severe heart condition, you certainly can play a lot of sports.

WHITE: I did not intend that this note should be read aloud. I do not know any reason why it should be public that I am ill, but I think probably one of the reasons why I suffered a heart attack was because I played so many sports, and so well. The heart attack which I suffered was last year. I am speaking of playing ping-pong, and I was a fair tennis player, and a pretty good ball player, many years prior to that. I hope that clears that up, Mr. Chairman.

THE CHAIRMAN: Yes, sir. [Applause.]

I would say that you had an athlete's heart. Go ahead, Mr. Stripling.

STRIPLING: Getting back to the question, Mr. White, whether you were in the Silvermaster basement, did you ever notice any photographic equipment?

WHITE: I do not recollect. I do not think I would have paid any attention to it. I am not at all interested in photography myself. I do not think I have snapped a picture in twenty years. It might have been; it might not. I do know, though, that Mr. [William L.] Ullmann [White's assistant at the Treasury Department and the member of the Silvermaster group who photographed stolen government documents] was interested in photography. I do know that. He had some splendid photographs in his home, which were, he said, done by him—Silvermaster—done by him, and they looked quite professional. And I also remember that many years prior to that, or as a result of that, I asked whether he would not take some pictures of my children, which he very generously did, and they are very excellent pictures. We still have them, and they are hanging in my bedroom.

STRIPLING: Mr. White, the names that I read to you a few moments ago, were the people that Elizabeth T. Bentley testified comprise the so-called Silvermaster group. A number of these people worked for you. I believe you admitted knowing all but one.

WHITE: Not admitted: affirmed, if you do not mind, Mr. Stripling.

STRIPLING: I will be glad to change the term. Would you tell me whether or not you have ever had any reason to suspect that any of those people were members of the Communist Party?

WHITE: No, except one; and if I may cite the occasion—

STRIPLING: Yes.

WHITE: It was either 1942 or 1943—I do not think it was as late as 1944; I think 1942 or 1943—Mr. Silvermaster spoke to me, saying that he was being asked to resign from the Board of Economic Warfare on the ground that he was being accused of being a Communist; and he asked whether I could not be of some assistance to get his name cleared. He had never impressed me as a Communist; he was an able economist and interested in world affairs. We had had many discussions.

I said to him—well, I was a little taken aback, and I said, "Well, are you a Communist?" He said, "No." I said "Well, what is there that you can give me or show me or what charges have been made? I cannot do anything for you unless I know something about your background, more than I did." He said he would send me a copy of a reply which he made, I think, to the Civil Service Commission. I am not quite sure.

He subsequently sent me a ten- or twenty-page—it was a fairly long—statement, in which there was, prefacing each paragraph, an allegation or a claim or a statement, apparently made by somebody. I would judge from the paper that he had access to the charge that was made. And then his reply was set up there.

After reading the reply it convinced me of the integrity of the man, and that he was not a Communist.

I then went to Mr. Herbert Gaston, who was Assistant Secretary of the Treasury, and on the Loyalty Board, and a fairer and more conscientious man never served the Government, as anybody who knew or who happened to know Mr. Herbert Gaston would testify. I went to him and I said that this man was being asked to resign from the Board—I think it was subsequent to that—and I said he was being asked to resign now.

I can well understand and thoroughly sympathize with the view that any slightest question of a man's being a Communist, he ought not to be in a position— ought not to hold a position where there was any confidential information passed; that even though there was no evidence or proof, a mere suspicion was enough. We were at war, and there was no need for that. I said that I was not interested in seeing him get his post back. In fact, I did not think he should.

I said that I understood that this record was such that he could not get his old post back with the Department of Agriculture, which was, I had presumed, nothing to do with any possible confidential information; and I said, unless there was evidence, it seemed to me that it would be a darned shame for a man to lose his livelihood and not be able to work for the government unless there was a case against him, and I said, "Mr. Gaston"—

or "Herbert," as I called him—"would you please look
into this and satisfy yourself as to the merits of the case."

Mr. Gaston said he would. Mr. Gaston subsequently
informed me and I think the man was cleared. He must
have been, because he got a job in the Department of
Agriculture. That was the only occasion in which there
was any question in my mind raised as to any of these
men that you mentioned being a Communist.

In the testimony that followed, White acknowledged to Stripling
that most of the alleged members of the Silvermaster group had
worked for him in the Treasury Department and that he had been
responsible—directly in some cases, indirectly in others—for their
employment there.

The subject then returned to Whittaker Chambers, and Congressman Richard Nixon joined the questioning.

STRIPLING: Mr. White, one of the members of the committee has asked me to show you a picture of Whittaker
Chambers.

WHITE: Yes.

STRIPLING: The picture I have here, one from *Time*
magazine of August 16, which picture was taken by
Thomas McAvoy of *Life*, and the other appeared in the
New York *Herald Tribune* of August 4, which is an
Acme Telefoto. I will show you these two pictures, and
ask you if you recall an individual who resembles Whittaker Chambers. [Showing witness two photographs.]

WHITE: I think I have seen that one [indicating].

STRIPLING: I should like to state, however, that according to our information that individual is much heavier now than he was in 1935 or 1936.

WHITE: This one, I think, I have seen [indicating]. No; I have no recollection of ever having met him. Of course, that is twelve or fourteen years ago.

THE CHAIRMAN: What was the answer?

WHITE: What is that, sir?

THE CHAIRMAN: What was the answer?

WHITE: I say I have no recollection of ever having met him. It was twelve or fifteen years ago. I must have met anywhere from five to ten thousand persons in the last fifteen years, but I have no recollection. It may be that he did meet me, and it may be that I did chat with him.

NIXON: In the event that you had met that individual, Mr. White, on, say, as many as three or four occasions, would you recollect whether you had or had not met him?

WHITE: The oftener I was supposed to have met him, the more nearly would it be that I would have remembered. It partly depends on where, what the conversation was. I should think so, three or four times, I do not know.

NIXON: Well, assuming that a meeting did occur on as many as four occasions, would your testimony be that you do not recollect having met this person?

WHITE: My testimony would have been the same. I do not recollect ever having met him. It is possible that I may have met a chap like that in any one of a dozen conferences or cocktail parties or meetings.

NIXON: Suppose you had met this individual on four occasions by himself, and were engaged in conversation with him, would you recollect whether you did or did not?

WHITE: I should think I would—I should think I would, but I am not sure.

NIXON: And you do not want to say then that if you had met him on three or four occasions, whether you do or not remember having met him?

WHITE: I do not recollect ever having met him.

NIXON: You do not recall having met any person who was known to you by the name of Carl during that period?

WHITE: No; I do not. Something I remember very definitely, though, judging from the papers, and I am quoting only from the papers, or referring to the papers, that the gentleman said that he met me and was convincing me or tried to convince me, either not to go into or leave—I do not remember precisely—the Communist Party or the

Communist ring. That, I would have remembered. And that I can affirm without any qualification or hesitation or shortness of memory or breath could not possibly have been so.

NIXON: I think it might be possible, Mr. White, that you are confusing the testimony that Mr. Chambers gave in regard to you, and that which he gave in regard to Alger Hiss. It was Mr. Hiss, who Mr. Chambers testified that he asked to leave the Communist Party, not you.

WHITE: Well, that is possible.

NIXON: There is no claim, in other words, by Mr. Chambers that you were asked to come into the party or out of the party.

WHITE: I am sorry, I did not read the testimony.

NIXON: I just wanted to have you understand that.

WHITE: I happened to be in the country most of the time, and the local papers do not give much coverage of the news.

NIXON: Your testimony is that you did not during the year 1935 or 1937—

WHITE: I do not recollect having met that individual.

NIXON: I am sorry, but I did not hear you. You what?

WHITE: I said I do not recollect having met the individual. I am merely repeating what I said before.

Stripling and Karl Mundt went on to question White about his relations with alleged members of the Silvermaster group, including his efforts to help Silvermaster himself retain his government employment after the latter had come under suspicion of having communist ties.

After further questioning and a short recess, Nixon resumed his inquiry into White's association with Whittaker Chambers.

NIXON: Mr. White, a moment ago I may have left an impression with you—I said a moment ago I may have left an impression with you in regard to the testimony of Mr. Chambers which, upon looking at the record, I found may have been incorrect. I indicated to you that Mr. Chambers had testified that he had gone to see Mr. Hiss and had requested that he leave the party, and that Mr. Hiss had refused.

As far as you are concerned, his testimony was not that he had requested that you leave the party, but that he did discuss with you the fact that he was leaving what he termed the Communist movement and that he advised apparently that you would do also.

Now, you can state categorically, I understand, that that is not true.

WHITE: Well, I do not remember whether anybody ever told me they were leaving the Communist movement. I think that would have stuck in my memory, but I very definitely can say that no one ever asked me to leave the movement, because I never belonged to it.

NIXON: As I say, there is a difference between party membership and maybe adherence to the tenets of the party, and I think that was the distinction Mr. Chambers was making in his testimony. His indication was not, in his testimony at that time, that you were actually a party member, you understand; that is the point that I wish to make.

WHITE: Well, my statement would go for a request that I cease being—what did you say—a first cousin to this movement?

NIXON: Whatever you like.

WHITE: Whatever you like to call it.

NIXON: In other words, the point I want to clear up is that you are stating for the record that at no time did this man by the name of Carl discuss with you the fact that he was leaving the Communist Party, and discuss also the matter of your, shall we say, ceasing to be a friend of the Communist Party—shall we put it that way.

WHITE: The first, certainly, not to my recollection. The second, I certainly would have remembered, and the answer is "No."

White was questioned further about his efforts to help Silvermaster clear his name. Then Chairman Thomas took up the accusations that had brought White before the committee.

THE CHAIRMAN: What charges have been made by any witness before this committee that prompted you to come and request that you appear as a witness?

WHITE: On Saturday a week ago, Al Gregory, an acquaintance, called me on the telephone and said that I had been accused of being the leader of a spy ring. I read in the next Sunday's paper testimony by a Miss Bentley and by—whether it was that same day or subsequently— Mr. Chambers of such charges, and naturally, I wanted to appear before this committee to clear my name insofar as it is possible to do so.

THE CHAIRMAN: You heard or read that you had been charged with being a leader of a spy ring?

WHITE: I heard that, and I think I read it, too, in the press.

THE CHAIRMAN: Who charged you with being the leader of a spy ring?

WHITE: Either or both, a Miss Bentley and a Mr. Whittaker Chambers.

THE CHAIRMAN: Mr. Chief Investigator, what charges were made against Mr. White?

WHITE: Other charges, if I might add.

THE CHAIRMAN: Against Mr. White; and what were they?

WHITE: That I stated in my preliminary statement that I had placed—

THE CHAIRMAN: By either Mr. Chambers or Miss Bentley.

WHITE: That I had placed in key posts or positions men whom I knew to be espionage agents for the purpose of furthering their work. That charge was repeated in the papers.

STRIPLING: Do you want me to read it?

THE CHAIRMAN: Yes.

STRIPLING: This is the testimony of July 31 of Elizabeth Bentley. She was referring to the people in the Silvermaster group who were in the Treasury. She was asked by Mr. Stripling:

Were there any other individuals in the Treasury Department who were working with your group?

Miss Bentley: With the Silvermaster group?

Mr. Stripling: Yes.

Bentley: Yes. Harry Dexter White.

Stripling: What was Mr. White's position?

Bentley: I believe he was Assistant Secretary of the Treasury, is that correct, or do you call him an Under Secretary, I am not sure.

Stripling: Assistant Secretary of the Treasury.

Mr. Chairman: The witness says she believes. What was he? We want to know.

Stripling: He was Assistant Secretary of the Treasury and head of Monetary Research, as I know.

Mr. Rankin: Is he a Communist?

Bentley: I do not know whether Mr. White was a card-carrying Communist or not.

Stripling: What was the extent of his cooperation with your group?

Bentley: He gave information to Mr. Silvermaster which was relayed to me.

THE CHAIRMAN: Did you ever give information to Mr. Silvermaster concerning the work of your department?

WHITE: We must have talked about the work in my department. I would never give him any secret or confidential information.

THE CHAIRMAN: Why not?

WHITE: I did not do it to anybody. I did not do it to anybody who was unauthorized. There were, of course, within the division scores of people who worked on problems.

THE CHAIRMAN: But you went to the extent of getting in touch with Mr. Gaston to get his name cleared because he had been charged with being a Communist, because he was a friend of yours.

WHITE: Precisely. I will do a lot for my friends, good friends, and that was the least any decent human being could do for a man whom we thought was innocent.

THE CHAIRMAN: Now, going back and recalling those days, did you ever recall Mr. Silvermaster asking you for any information that might be of a secret nature or such that you should not give it out?

WHITE: No, no; I never have. In those years we discussed a good deal about Germany and Hitler's activity, and the possibilities of war, and then, after the war, the possibilities of success, those problems. We discussed economic problems; we ranged the field pretty well. I do not remember his ever asking me for any confidential information, because it would be none of his business.

THE CHAIRMAN: If you were shown a photostatic copy of a Communist dues-paying card or a Communist membership card with Mr. Silvermaster's name on it, would you believe that Mr. Silvermaster was a Communist?

WHITE: Well, it certainly would be strong presumptive evidence that he was. I do not know whether those things are framed; yes, I should think it would be that. If that is evidence before the court, I would accept it. The court is in a better position than I am.

THE CHAIRMAN: How many of these other people whose names have been mentioned here today by Mr. Stripling either worked under you or with you or that you helped in some way or another?

WHITE: Well, I can remember some of the names, but I do not remember all.

THE CHAIRMAN: The names that you can recall.

WHITE: Well, Frank Coe I have described. [Coe was a Treasury colleague whom White acknowledged knowing well.]

THE CHAIRMAN: Yes.

WHITE: He came to the Treasury at the same time I did. Harold Glasser, I employed some ten or twelve years ago, and he came from another government department. Bill Taylor worked for me—who were some of the others? Where the checks are?

STRIPLING: Blue checks.

WHITE: Red checks would be more appropriate.

THE CHAIRMAN: That is the best statement you have made.

WHITE: I added it from your point of view.

THE CHAIRMAN: I did not hear the latter part.

WHITE: I will run down the list.

STRIPLING: Perhaps I should read the ones that I asked you about.

WHITE: Please do that.

STRIPLING: Just to refresh your memory. Solomon Adler.

WHITE: He worked in the Division.

THE CHAIRMAN: What was that name?

WHITE: Solomon Adler.

STRIPLING: Norman Bursler.

WHITE: He did not work for me.

STRIPLING: Frank Coe, you have mentioned.

WHITE: I have mentioned him.

STRIPLING: Lauchlin Currie.

WHITE: Lauchlin Currie you know about that.

STRIPLING: Sonia Gold.

WHITE: She worked for the Division for a while.

STRIPLING: William J. Gold.

WHITE: No.

STRIPLING: Irving Kaplan.

WHITE: I do not think so. The reason I hesitate there is that we have a branch, a sort of subsidiary, that was called Foreign Exchange control, in which there were several hundred employees. I have a vague recollection that he might have worked for them for a time. I am not sure. The records, I think, will show that. He did not work in the Division of Monetary Research.

STRIPLING: George Silverman.

WHITE: George Silverman did not work for us, but when we were establishing the Foreign Exchange, we were very short-handed for excellent statisticians, and in my judgment George Silverman is among the best economic statisticians. I asked his superior whether he could not release him for a couple of months to get started—to help us get started, and I think his superior did, and we got him over there.

STRIPLING: William H. Taylor.

WHITE: He worked for us.

STRIPLING: William L. Ullmann.

WHITE: He worked for us.

THE CHAIRMAN: What was that last name?

WHITE: Ullmann.

STRIPLING: That is all. Victor Perlo.

WHITE: Victor Perlo I explained. [Perlo was a Treasury official whom White said he knew but not well. Perlo had testified before HUAC earlier in the week, refusing to state under oath that he was not a member of the Communist Party.]

THE CHAIRMAN: Mr. White, of all the persons who have been mentioned at these hearings to date, nine or ten have worked in your Department, and in addition to that, two others are friends of yours, and one is a very close friend.

Now, how do you account for this?

WHITE: That is one of those "when did you stop beating your wife" questions.

THE CHAIRMAN: Not exactly.

WHITE: But let me answer. I did not know whether there were nine or ten. There may have been.

THE CHAIRMAN: Well, say eight or nine.

WHITE: It does not matter for our purposes whether there were seven or eleven. In the first place, all of these men that worked for us are what I would call class A and some class AA economists in the field in which they were interested. We had working for us, or we have hired, or I have hired, or my assistants have employed rather than hired, probably over a hundred economists during the course of these years, well over a hundred economists. At least one of these men was there when I came, there were several of them who came just the way they always come, through Civil Service, or through the Employment Bureau, and their qualifications were suitable.

Ullmann, I employed knowing him, myself. I would have been glad to employ George Silverman, but he would not have worked for me. We could not have paid him enough. I asked him. Several of them were employed by assistant directors, recommended, and it would have gotten my approval.

THE CHAIRMAN: Well, maybe I did not phrase my question correctly.

WHITE: Would you mind rephrasing it?

THE CHAIRMAN: I will put the question in a different way.

WHITE: Do, because I have not the slightest intention of dodging it.

THE CHAIRMAN: No. Don't you think it is strange that of the persons, all the persons mentioned, either by Miss Bentley or by Whittaker Chambers, that of those persons mentioned, at least eight or nine of them, possibly ten, worked under you, and two others are friends of yours?

WHITE: Well, it is certainly disconcerting, but I would not say it is strange. We had probably the largest economic department; those are economists, and most of them are, and they are economists, most of them, in a special field in which the logical place for them to go would be either one of two places, the Federal Reserve Board, and the Treasury; and the Treasury at that time was expanding rapidly because we were given responsibilities far in excess of anything we had; and we needed all the good people we could possibly get; and I have called up my colleagues that I have known in the profession, not one, but a dozen of them, and I said, "Would you please send me the best men you had, so that we could get them," and this got around, I am sure, and anybody who was good who wanted a job, he would come to the Treasury, and if he was good, and I think I am a pretty good judge of the competence in that field, he got the job.

Congressman McDowell was the last member of the committee to question White, focusing on White's relationship with William Ullmann, Silvermaster's photographer. McDowell's conclusion made it clear that White had failed to exonerate himself in the eyes of the committee.

McDOWELL: Well, I have no further questions, Dr. White, but in view of the very noble statements you have made here about the rights of humans, star-chamber proceedings, and so forth, all of which I agree with, and I am sure the other members do, too, but you have testified that you knew Mr. Perlo, Mr. Ullmann, Mr. Silverman, and Mr. Silvermaster and Mr. Kramer.

WHITE: That is right, sir.

McDOWELL: In the case of one or two of them, you have testified that they were friends, good friends, and you are willing to defend them, and you have proven that you would defend them.

WHITE: That is right, sir.

McDOWELL: In case we proved that these men are all part of an espionage ring, your place in history is going to be changed considerably, would you not think?

WHITE: I certainly think that I would not profit by having as close friends people who have been of disservice to their Government.

McDOWELL: That is all, Mr. Chairman.

The hearing concluded with Stripling's reading into the record a portion of Whittaker Chambers's testimony before HUAC ten days earlier.

STRIPLING: This testimony was given on August 3 by Whittaker Chambers.

Stripling: Mr. Chambers, Miss Bentley testified last Saturday and she named Harry Dexter White as a person who worked with the espionage group. Did you know Harry Dexter White?

Chambers: Yes; I did.

Stripling: Is Harry Dexter White a Communist? Was he a Communist, to your knowledge?

Chambers: I can't say positively that he was a registered member of the Communist Party, but he certainly was a fellow traveler so far within the fold that his not being a Communist would be a mistake on both sides.

Stripling: Did you go to Harry Dexter White when you left the Communist Party and ask him also to leave the party?

Chambers: I did.

Stripling: You considered him to be a Communist Party member, then?

Chambers: Well, I accepted an easy phrasing. I didn't ask him to leave the Communist Party, but to break away from the Communist movement.

Stripling: What did he tell you?

Chambers: He left me apparently in a very agitated frame of mind, and I thought I had succeeded. Apparently I did not.

CHAPTER 13

CHECK
AND
CHECKMATE

Harry Dexter White walked out of the House Un-American Activities Committee hearing a dead man.

When he brought down the house with his "American Creed" speech, it looked like he would carry the day. Then Robert Stripling showed him the photographs of Whittaker Chambers, and White realized that Chambers was Carl. Richard Nixon picked right up on it, probably from the expression on White's face when he saw the pictures. Nixon got White so confused that when Nixon seemed to admit that he could have confused White with Alger Hiss—another Soviet agent—White fell for it. Karl Mundt established that White had cleared accused Soviet agents of suspicion on his authority, without an independent investigation by the FBI or even by the State Department's security officer. HUAC even knew about Silvermaster's basement darkroom, where classified documents were photographed for the Soviets. It was all over. The hearing that White himself had requested turned out to be a catastrophe. The committee now knew—or at least had good reason to suspect—that he was a traitor. But they did not know that he was one of the most important traitors in American history—the man who had triggered the attack on Pearl Harbor before the U.S. was ready for war, and who nearly handed over Germany's formidable industrial plant to Stalin. All they needed now was to hear from Jonathan Mitchell how White had gone half-crazy, declaring the decline and fall of Christianity and capitalism and extolling "the Russian system" as the wave of the future. Harry Dexter White was finished making history.

On the train back to his farm in New Hampshire, White took stock of his options. Once Whittaker Chambers confronted him, an indictment would be only a matter of time. Roosevelt was dead. Morgenthau was gone and discredited. The misconceived Morgenthau Plan had been replaced by the Marshall Plan, which, by building a free and prosperous West Germany, was erecting a bulwark against Soviet ambitions in Europe. The shift in foreign policy from anti-Nazi to anti-Soviet meant that White could not expect any support or sympathy. He was one step away from being tried for treason, and he knew it.

During the Bretton Woods Conference in 1944, Harry Dexter White, like John Maynard Keynes, had been on heart-attack watch, and the physicians had prescribed digitalis for any future heart trouble. Digitalis, in small doses, could strengthen a failing heart. In large doses, digitalis could trigger a heart attack. White had experienced heart troubles during the hearings in Washington. Once he was back in New York City, he saw his doctor. His heart had gotten him through the hearings in Washington—even through the shock of Whittaker Chambers's photograph—but it would not take him much farther.

By coincidence, Hollywood had already scripted a way out of White's predicament for him. In Fritz Lang's 1944 film *noir* hit *The Woman in the Window*, Edward G. Robinson plays a respected academic with a wife and children who blunders into a love triangle and becomes entangled in murder and blackmail. Robinson's character, Professor Richard Wanley, could have been modeled on Harry Dexter White. A physician friend of Wanley's prescribes what appears to be digitalis, assuming that his lassitude is due to heart strain. A little will perk you up, he tells Wanley, but don't take too much or you'll be dead in twenty minutes. Wanley ingests the whole bottle.

In *Leave Her to Heaven*, an enormous film *noir* hit released the following year, Gene Tierney's character attempts to disguise her suicide through cremation. After taking poison, she requests cremation on her deathbed but has inserted an order for an autopsy and burial in her will (thus framing a perceived rival in love for murder).

On the train back to the farm at Fitzwilliam, New Hampshire, Harry Dexter White—an officer and a gentleman for the Allies in World War I—made up his mind. His wife apparently did not know the extent of his treason, and his daughters and the rest of the family knew nothing. The family could be protected if he did the right thing. He gulped down the digitalis and waited.... But it took longer than twenty minutes.

The chest pains and the blurred vision and flashing lights started while White was still on the train. The next day, he was seen by Dr. George S. Emerson, the elderly general practitioner in Fitzwilliam, who diagnosed heart trouble. Dr. Emerson could not do much. He saw White twice during the heart failure, but White died at home on August 16, 1948, three days after his testimony before HUAC.

Emerson—a kindly old man, and anxious to spare the family's feelings—reported that there was nothing about White's death to indicate suicide:

> [White] said that while on the train [on August 14] he had severe attacks of terrible pain in his chest. The next day I saw him twice. The second time he called me, I wasn't here, and while they tried to reach me, they finally got Dr. Herbert E. Flewelling of Peterboro, then a young doctor in Jaffrey. We got there about the same time. He brought his electrocardiograph machine and we took an electro-cardiogram. It showed definite heart trouble.
>
> He said nothing about the trouble he'd been through in Washington and I didn't know about it at the time. The next day, the 16th, I saw him twice but I left before he died. There's nothing to this suicide talk. I don't believe he could have died from an overdose of digitalis. That night when they came to get the body, I was on a maternity case in Keene, and they got me to sign the death certificate.

Dr. Emerson had logged the cause of death as "coronary heart attack due to disease of coronary arteries and heart." Dr. Emerson, of course, was unaware that White had been a Soviet agent or that the HUAC hearing had uncovered his relationship with a known Soviet courier and his protection of other Soviet agents. Dr. Flewelling did not know this either, and he said that he "remembered the case well because of all the hullabaloo afterwards. I'll try to look up the cardiogram. We both felt strongly at the time that it was a typical death caused by heart trouble. I remember distinctly it was an abnormal cardiogram definitely indicating he had heart trouble. He was having a very severe episode of pain. It was a very definite thing, of the kind we see often. I saw nothing about the case at the time that seemed suspicious to me, such as taking poison. I saw nothing in the cardiogram that would suggest taking too much digitalis."

Taking too much digitalis on top of an existing heart condition would trigger exactly the symptoms that White displayed. Neither physician understood White's motivation for suicide—to save his family from disgrace and to cover acts of betrayal far more damaging than any that Whittaker Chambers knew about.

If it was a suicide, the evidence was soon destroyed. The body was taken to Boston by J. S. Waterman & Son, with a burial permit signed by William M. Blodgett, town clerk of Fitzwilliam. White received a Jewish funeral at Waterman's chapel, with Rabbi Irving Mandel of Boston's Temple Israel officiating. About thirty-five people attended. The body was then cremated at the Forest Hills cemetery in Jamaica Plain. Cremation is prohibited by Jewish law, but Harry Dexter White had long since secretly forsaken his Judaism for Marxism. And cremation prevents an autopsy.

Suicide of one type or another had also been the rule in Japan. Fumimaro Konoye, whose proposed meeting with Roosevelt might have avoided World War II in the Pacific, killed himself with a cyanide capsule at the end of 1945. Hideki Tojo, Konoye's successor as prime minister, had a physician draw a target on his chest and shot himself four times. He survived, incredibly enough, with the care of an American physician and transfusions of American blood, to stand trial for war crimes in place of the emperor, who had sanctioned the attack on Pearl Harbor to save himself and his dynasty.

Hirohito had been the designated villain of Pearl Harbor in Frank Capra's *Why We Fight* films, shown to every U.S. serviceman during basic training. Late in the war, the government prevailed upon the anthropologist Ruth Benedict to write *The Chrysanthemum and the Sword*, a study of Japanese culture. Benedict, who had never lived in Japan and could not speak or read Japanese, argued that keeping Hirohito on the throne was a political necessity, and her book became influential. American anxiety over the prospect of Japan falling under Soviet domination meant that the emperor stayed.

Tomoyuki Yamashita and Masaharu Homma had already been executed for "war crimes" in 1946, to the horror of their American defense counsel, who realized that neither man had been guilty as charged. Yamashita, "The Tiger of Malaya," had beaten the British at Singapore and bluffed them into surrender though they outnumbered him three to one. Handed command of the Philippines when the Americans landed in 1944, Yamashita—an Army general—had failed to prevent the "Rape of Manila" as Japanese Naval troops not under his control rampaged and murdered an estimated one hundred thousand civilians who rose to help the Americans. Some of the dead were Filipino guerillas, themselves merciless to the Japanese, but many were harmless civilians. Yamashita was hanged.

Masaharu Homma, the nominal commander of Bataan in 1942, was charged with fomenting the atrocities at the beginning of the campaign. He too argued that he lacked the authority to prevent the abuse and murder of prisoners and in fact had not learned what had happen until two months later. Though his American defense team thought he made a strong case, his American judges pronounced him guilty. When Homma's wife asked Douglas MacArthur for clemency in excellent English, MacArthur decreed that Homma, the man who had chased him out of the Philippines, could be shot rather than hanged—but not in uniform. On the flight back to Japan, a stewardess offered Homma's wife a U.S. Army blanket to keep warm in the frigid aircraft. She spotted the letters "U.S." on the blanket and threw it into the aisle.

Homma gave away his leather goods—expensive in Japan—to his defense team, and tried to cheer up the leery enlisted men in his firing squad. Most of the correspondents who had covered his trial in Manila had expected him to get off, because the evidence was based at least in part on hysteria and propaganda. When Homma was offered a blindfold before his execution, he dryly remarked that if he had been afraid of guns, he would have gone into some other line of work. Just before being shot, he was offered a couple of beers. He shared them with the American kids in the firing squad to calm them down.

Tojo was somewhat more obdurate. Unlike Homma, who had served on the Western Front during World War I with British, French, and American forces, Tojo knew little about whites. He had, it is true, argued that the captured Doolittle aviators, who had bombed Japan in April 1942, could not be executed as war criminals, even though they struck two schools and a hospital along with factories—they were simply soldiers following orders and thus entitled to protection as prisoners of war. The Japanese courts disagreed and shot those flyers who were over twenty-one, after tying them to crosses to facilitate their passage to Heaven and get rid of the ghosts.

The "war criminals" with whom Tojo was tried at the International Military Tribunal for the Far East at Tokyo were a very mixed bag. During the infamous Bataan Death March, Japanese and Korean soldiers—some American survivors said the Koreans in the Japanese Army were the worst—had indeed murdered and brutalized prisoners. But many of these were ignorant peasants, handed a death sentence with their draft notices and eager for some displaced aggression. And some American POWs, especially the bitter recent draftees, brought a portion of their troubles on themselves. They thought defeat and capture had absolved them of their military status. The young Americans who did not want to be soldiers broke discipline, expecting to be ignored or shouted at by the Japanese; they were executed instead. Others foolishly treated their Japanese captors with the same racial contempt they showed to "people of color" at home—and received savage beatings in return.

The Bataan Death March was a series of premature deaths by murder or neglect, but it was not an organized, premeditated massacre. It was a badly coordinated attempt to relocate a broken, abandoned, and angry Army where discipline, morale, and logistics had collapsed with the sudden outbreak of war. Both sides behaved badly. When escaped Americans reported the outrages in January 1944, the American death toll was reported as 5,200, and Army propaganda posters urged Americans to "stay on the job until every murdering Jap is wiped out." The actual death toll was between 600 and 650—many of them murdered, some simply dead from exhaustion. By 1980, survivors on both sides, American and Japanese, were holding bibulous reunions where they hugged and swapped hats.

General Iwane Matsui, a lifelong friend of China, had been flat on his back with malaria when his soldiers unleashed the Rape of Nanking in 1937. Matsui was indignant, did what he could to palliate the looting and the rapes, and then collapsed again. John Rabe, the German businessman whom the Chinese declared "a living Buddha" for breaking up rapes and robbery with the help of the Japanese officers he dragged along with him, confirmed that numerous rapes and murders had taken place—by dim-witted Japanese soldiers who turned into brigands once they got drunk on looted liquor. Japanese medical officers meanwhile roamed the Safety Zone looking for experienced girls who wanted to make some money, and telling the obvious virgins to keep themselves clean, get an education, and grow up to be good Chinese mothers. Matsui, once he got off his back, instituted sanitary proceedings and rationing to feed the survivors, who vastly outnumbered the victims.

Matsui was nevertheless charged with war crimes after Japan's defeat and confronted with numbers supplied by the Chinese which were enormously exaggerated. American, British, German, and Danish sources had reported between 17,000 and 50,000 Chinese dead from battle and execution, and suggested that casual murder and rape were fairly common. The Chinese claimed 300,000 murders and 20,000 rapes. The current Chinese figure is 400,000 murders and 80,000 rapes. Those were the numbers that went into the books. Fumiko Hayashi—a female Japanese author, a fearless feminist, and a literary Bohemian—and Ashihei Hino—a Japanese corporal from a leftist background—both described the Japanese occupation of China in what seemed to be unflinchingly honest accounts. Both felt that despite the brutality of the war, the Chinese were better off under a harsh Japanese occupation than they were under the chaos of the wars between the Chinese Nationalists and the Chinese Communists. All records confirm that there were more Chinese alive in Nanking in 1945 than in 1937. Matsui was sentenced to death for the Rape of Nanking.

Kenji Doihara—"Lawrence of Manchuria" to his British admirers—was tried for plotting aggressive war against China, when in fact the Marco Polo Bridge Incident of 1937 was the result of bungling on both sides. Doihara, a flamboyant adventurer and swordsman, fluent in Chinese, had always been pro-British and pro-American. He was also an anti-communist and had strongly opposed the war with the United States. He too was sentenced to death.

The strangest name of all on the list of defendants at the Tokyo Trials was Koki Hirota, "the man in the ordinary suit," who was dragged into the cabinet after the junior officers' uprising of February 1936 to try to conciliate the distressed working people of Japan. Hirota had long been out of power during the negotiations that led up to Pearl Harbor and had advised against the attack. He knew when he was indicted that he would be sacrificed to save Hirohito's throne and to obscure the fact that the Japanese had tried frantically to back away from attacking Pearl Harbor. He was not unduly upset. His wife, who had sold her jewelry to buy food for their children, had died from malnutrition. One of his sons had committed suicide because he had done badly on his exams. When another of Hirota's sons visited him during his trial, Hirota remained cheerful.

"I imagine you're prepared for the worst, aren't you, father?"

"Of course I am."

Hirota told his son that he looked forward to meeting his wife, his own parents, and his dead son in the next world, and was not afraid of being hanged, much as he might have preferred a bullet or beheading. "I've been nearly throttled to death any number of times at judo," Hirota told his son. "So I know it's not at all an unpleasant way of dying."

"They say you have to walk up thirteen steps, and at the top of the steps a board gives way," his son said. "Mind you don't slip on the steps."

"I know, I know," Hirota replied calmly.

The French and Dutch judges at the war crimes trials argued against a death sentence for Koki Hirota, and even his American prosecutor, Joseph Keenan, was surprised when it was imposed.

Hirota watched the Tokyo Trials with a certain detachment. He was not surprised when Hideki Tojo, who had started to tell what really happened before Pearl Harbor, was warned in a whisper that if he continued, his family would lose their pension. If, on the other hand, the emperor were not implicated, the pension would be doubled. Tojo complied. He took the blame and the double pension for his family.

Six months after Harry Dexter White, the real author of the attack on Pearl Harbor, took his leave of this world, the Japanese "war lords" who had struck Pearl Harbor to honor their pledge and save their emperor from revolution faced the rope in Tokyo.

As the first group of Japanese generals was led off to be hanged, Iwane Matsui called the three rounds of "Banzai"—"Tenno Hekka Banzai"—"May the emperor live ten thousand years." Hideki Tojo, Kenji Doihara, and the other scapegoats joined in the cheer. Koki Hirota did not cheer.

"Listen… they were doing *manzai* just now, weren't they?" Hirota dryly asked the Buddhist chaplain. *Manzai* are Japanese buffoonery, skits among low-life comedians or—with a slight change in pronunciation—Korean-language cheers. Koki Hirota prayed but he did not cheer. He knew better.

The one justice on the tribunal who voted for acquittal, Radhabinod Pal of India, split the difference. Many of the Japanese "Class B" war crimes against Asian civilians and Anglo-American POWs were "devilish and fiendish," he said, though Nanking was exaggerated for propaganda purposes. Japan's attempt to take over the world at Pearl Harbor, however, was a fake: "Even contemporary historians could think that as far as the present war, the Principality of Monaco, the Grand Duchy of Luxembourg would have taken up arms against the United States on receipt of such a note as the State Department sent the Japanese Government on the eve of Pearl Harbor." The Japanese have erected a shrine to Justice Pal, but his book-length dissent from the Tokyo verdict has never been available in the United States or the United Kingdom.

Harry Dexter White deflected the verdict of history with his sudden death. Liberal historians remembered the brave little man who stood up to the red-baiting thugs of HUAC as a hero of democracy. Nixon himself believed that J. Parnell Thomas was destroyed because he dared to humiliate Harry Dexter White with his crack about an "athlete's heart"—a pun on "athlete's foot"—a few days before White's "heart attack." For the next three decades, especially after Senator Joseph McCarthy's scatter-shot attacks gave anti-communism a bad name, White was seen as a victim of paranoid right-wing radicals and sleazy politicians. White's brother Nathan, who seems to have believed that Harry was entirely innocent, defiantly assembled all the congressional testimony and news clippings in a privately printed book, *Harry D. White—Loyal American*. White's widow left his papers to Princeton University. The May 1941 and November 1941 memoranda, along with the "thirty blood-stained pieces of gold" letter urging the president to shun Japan's last-minute peace overtures, are preserved in the Seeley G. Mudd Manuscript Library.

The truth about White was revealed quite unexpectedly. Vitalii Pavlov, having retired in 1990 as a lieutenant general of the KGB, encountered an attack on Harry Dexter White by Congressman Hamilton Fish, who was one of the first to call White a traitor. To Pavlov, a Marxist true believer to the end, White was a hero who had come to the aid of the Soviet Union in its darkest hour. In 1996, he published the story of their fateful meeting at the Old Ebbitt

Grill and White's mission to provoke a war between the United States and Japan in *Operation Snow: Half a Century at KGB Foreign Intelligence*. Never translated into English, Pavlov's book clinches the case that started with Whittaker Chambers and Elizabeth Bentley and continued with the VENONA decrypts. White was indeed a Soviet spy, wielding enormous influence at the highest levels of government at one of the most critical junctures in American history.

Harry Dexter White, acting under orders of Soviet intelligence, pulled the strings by which Cordell Hull and Stanley Hornbeck handed the Japanese an ultimatum that was tantamount to a declaration of war—when both the Japanese cabinet and the U.S. military were desperately eager for peace. White could not have done it without the unwitting assistance of Stanley Hornbeck, Henry Morgenthau Jr., and Dean Acheson. Though each of these men had his own agenda, none of them was a communist, and in fact they all had some anti-communist credentials. They simply had other concerns that came before the best interests of the United States, and they lacked the knowledge or wisdom to stand in the way of the clever subversion of national security. Harry Dexter White knew exactly what he was doing. The man himself remains a mystery, but the documents speak for themselves. Harry Dexter White gave us Pearl Harbor.

ACKNOWLEDGMENTS

I gratefully acknowledge my staff of linguistic and cultural translators: Shizuko Masuda—Countess Obo, also known as Suzie Koster, my Japanese and written Chinese translator—who translated rare vintage newspapers, the précis of the Mitsuo Fuchida memoirs, and notes from contemporary Japanese researchers; InHye Lee—an ethnic Korean who grew up in Uzbekistan, Moscow, and the United States—my Russian-language translator, who provided the first English translation of Vitalii Pavlov's *Operation Snow*; Jessica Mok—an ethnic Korean who grew up in Japan, Korea, and the United States—who provided the Korean-language translations of material mostly from Dosan Press, known to most Koreans but completely unknown in English. I did my own sparse

French and German translations of some background works. While the Japanese, Russian, and Korean translations are now available in English for the first time, most of my sources have long been available in English and may be checked against official U.S. documents. Harry Dexter White's widow donated his notes to the Seeley G. Mudd Manuscript Library at Princeton University, and his brother self-published a book containing all the relevant testimony before Congress.

One of the first and best editors I ever worked with was Len Cacutt of Marshall Cavendish in the United Kingdom, a fireman during the London Blitz and later an air gunner in the Royal Air Force. When I asked this double survivor of Nazi outrages against his own country, which he defended with great courage, what he really thought of the origins of wars, he replied, "All wars are produced by politicians for their own benefits, and it's always Joe Soap who gets it right in the neck. It doesn't matter whether Joe Soap is British or American or German or French or even Japanese. He's the one who gets it in the neck."

—John Koster

A NOTE ON SOURCES

My opening chapter, "Meeting of Masterminds," is based on *Operation Snow: Half a Century at KGB Foreign Intelligence* by Vitalii Pavlov, retired lieutenant-general of the KGB, published in Russian in 1996 and never translated into English. InHye Lee, who grew up in Russian-language schools in Uzbekistan and Moscow, provided an original translation, which John Czop checked against the Polish translation of Pavlov's book. Pavlov provides all the colorful details of the first meeting. Herbert Romerstein, the co-author with Eric Breindel of *The Venona Secrets*, describes the same meeting (pp. 29–44), though not in the same detail, as do Jerrold and Leona Schechter in *Sacred Secrets*. Romerstein also establishes (pp. 520–521, notes) that the Tanaka Memorial was a

Soviet forgery, not Chinese. Allen Weinstein and Alexander Vassiliev provide excellent background on Soviet espionage in the United States in *The Haunted Wood*.

Details of Harry Dexter White's relationship with Whittaker Chambers come from *Witness*, in which Chambers reports that he believed he had persuaded White to drop out of the communist movement (pp. 67–68), describes his work as White's courier (pp. 383–384) before Chambers broke with the Communist Party after the unexplained disappearance of Juliet Stuart Poyntz, and provides an overview of Soviet espionage, including the stories of the Oriental rugs and misdirected gifts of vodka and caviar (pp. 414–434). The Charley Project, an online missing-persons database, contains information about the investigation of Poyntz's disappearance.

The most incriminating book on Harry Dexter White, ironically, is *Harry D. White—Loyal American* by his brother, Nathan White, privately published in 1956. This book provides photostats and verbatim texts of the memoranda in which White takes a precocious interest in Japan's oil supply (pp. 81–97), White's ferocious response to Jonathan Mitchell (pp. 232–245), the entire text of White's statement before the House Un-American Activities Committee (pp. 347–381), and a number of other anecdotes from family and old newspaper sources. White's government papers, at the Seeley G. Mudd Manuscript Library at Princeton University, include the full texts of the May Memorandum, the November Memorandum, and the one-page letter he wrote for Henry Morgenthau Jr.'s signature to prevent any concessions that might deflect Japan's decision to attack Pearl Harbor. The Mudd Library file also contains articles from *Time* and the *Saturday Evening Post* that describe White's passing of documents to the USSR late in the war.

The Sino-Japanese conflicts that foreshadowed White's use of China (rather than the Soviet Union) to influence President Roosevelt are covered from opposite perspectives in *Edgar Snow's China* (from the viewpoint of an American communist sympathizer) and *War Criminal: The Life and Death of Hirota Koki* by Saburo Shiroyama. Opposing views of Nanking are found in *The Rape of Nanking* by Iris Chang, *What Really Happened in Nanking* by Masaaki Tanaka, and *Hidden Horrors: Japanese War Crimes in World War II* by Yuki Tanaka. Edgar Snow's reported death toll of 42,000 is probably closer to reality than either Masaaki Tanaka's outright denial or Chang's hyperbole. The eyewitness account that John Rabe (a soft Nazi) recorded in his diary, later published as *The Good Man of Nanking*, is closer to Snow's (a soft communist) and Frank Tillman Durdin's (an honest Texan respected by both the Chinese and the Japanese for his integrity) than to either Chang's or Masaaki Tanaka's.

David Bergamini describes the events of 2/26 in *Japan's Imperial Conspiracy*, which credits Hirohito with more intelligence than he deserves but cites some of the documents that show that the rebel officers were idealistic pan-Asians and anti-communists rather than Nipponese Nazis bent on world conquest. Wikipedia has a full account of the February 26 Incident. The article was obviously written by a Japanese for whom English is a second language, but numerous documents, photos, and a list of the names of the ringleaders with the sentences imposed on them complete the picture of the event Hirohito did not want to see replayed. I have also relied on Shiroyama's account of the February 26 Incident, of Hirota's appointment as a reform-minded prime minister, and the organization of the Anti-Comintern Pact (pp. 129–162).

Kilsoo Haan's translation of *How Japan Plans to Win*, based on Matsuo Kinoaki's Japanese original, provides a look at Japan's war plans and, while conjuring up the air of menace that Haan wanted with its cover design, confirms the obvious—the Japanese felt menaced by the United States and had no plans for a landing on the North American continent. The deficiencies of Japanese tanks and trucks made obvious by the Nomonhan Incident are described in detail in Alvin Coox's book *Nomonhan: Japan against Russia, 1939*.

James Otto Richardson, another honest Texan, depicts the events leading up to the attack in *On the Treadmill to Pearl Harbor*. The last two-thirds of the book describe Richardson's perception that an unnecessary threat to Japan would lead to a war for which the United States was not ready. (Pages 251–436 are especially important and full of details, telegrams, letters, and statistics.) This essential book, published by the Naval History Division of the Department of the Navy in 1973, is the most important account of the navy's perspective. Husband Kimmel, in *Admiral Kimmel's Story*, also provides details about his attempts to provide adequate reconnaissance in advance of the attack. In *The Final Secret of Pearl Harbor*, Rear Admiral Robert Theobald shows how decoded Japanese messages clearly indicated that war was approaching and questions why the White House failed to warn the Pacific Fleet in time to give the sailors, marines, and soldiers on Oahu a fighting chance. Admiral Edward Layton, a U.S. intelligence officer who spoke Japanese, adds to the evidence of early warnings and considers Soviet complicity in *And I Was There*.

The double-page pictogram from *United States News* of October 31, 1941, which threatened Japan with incendiary air raids, is reproduced in Michael Sherry's *The Rise of American Air Power*. This work is also my source for George Marshall's pre-war threat of incendiary attacks on Japanese civilians. *Pearl Harbor Extra*, which reproduces newspaper front pages from the collection of Eric C. Caren, reveals a crescendo of warnings beginning December 1 and reaching a climax in the three days before the attack.

The file on the Korean patriot Kilsoo Haan at the American Heritage Center of the University of Wyoming contains documentation of Haan's attempts to warn U.S. officials of the impending attack and confirming responses on official stationery. Other accounts from the Korean underground were translated by Jessica Mok from Korean originals.

The two-page questionnaire seeking target information about Pearl Harbor and Oahu that the double agent Dusko Popov showed to the FBI is reproduced in his autobiography, *Spy/Counterspy*.

The desperate Japanese cabinet meeting that approved the attack is recounted in Shiroyama's *War Criminal*, most recently reprinted in 1990 (pp. 210–211). My mother-in-law, Toyoko Obo, and her family were well acquainted with the Hideki Tojo family; they knew Koki Hirota tangentially and Fumimaro Konoye at least by insider gossip. Their knowledge contributed to the account.

In *The FBI-KGB War*, Robert J. Lamphere provides an excellent technical description of how Meredith Gardner decoded the VENONA transcripts (pp. 78–86) and a good overview of Soviet espionage in the United States.

The account of White's death and funeral is based on *Harry Dexter White: A Study in Paradox* by David Rees (pp. 416–418). Despite Dr. Emerson's chivalrous attempt to shield the family, newspapers at the time reported an overdose of digitalis.

The amusing last words of General Masaharu Homma at his execution and his wife's response to the offer of a U.S. Army blanket are virtual folklore in Japan and alluded to in *Bridge to the*

Sun by Gwen Terasaki. Koki Hirota's ironic remarks at his own hanging in 1948 are quoted in Shiroyama's book (pp. 286–299). The summation of the Tokyo Trials is based on the Wikipedia article on Justice Radhabinod Pal. The text of Justice Pal's dissenting opinion is available online at http://www.sdh-fact.com/CL02_1/65_S4.pdf.

In conclusion, I thank my Japanese language translator, Shizuko Obo Koster, author of *Hachi-Ko: The Samurai Dog*, my Russian-language translator, InHye Lee, and my Korean-language translator and computer expert, Jessica Mok, for helping me put the pieces of this puzzle together. I hope the result will foster understanding between peoples and peace on earth.

BIBLIOGRAPHY

BOOKS

Andrew, Christopher, and Oleg Gordievsky. *KGB: The Inside Story*. New York: HarperCollins, 1990.

Andrew, Christopher, and Vasili Mitrokhin. *The Sword and the Shield: The Mitrokhin Archive and the Secret History of the KGB*. New York: Basic Books, 1999.

Armor, John, and Peter Wright. *Manzanar*. New York: Times Books, 1988 (photographs by Ansel Adams, commentary by John Hersey).

Bacque, James. *Other Losses: An Investigation into the Mass Deaths of German Prisoners at the Hands of the French and Americans after World War II*, 3rd ed. Vancouver: Talonbooks, 2011.

Behr, Edward. *Hirohito: Behind the Myth*. New York: Random House, 1989.

Berg, A. Scott. *Lindbergh*. New York: G. P. Putnam's Sons, 1998.

Bergamini, David. *Japan's Imperial Conspiracy*. New York: William Morrow & Co., 1971.

Bix, Herbert P. *Hirohito and the Making of Modern Japan*. New York: Harper, 2000.

Blackbeard, Bill, and Martin Williams. *The Smithsonian Collection of Newspaper Comics*. Washington: Smithsonian Institution, 1977.

Brimner, Larry Dane. *Voices from the Camps: Internment of Japanese Americans during World War II*. New York: Franklin Watts, 1994.

Buchanan, Patrick J. *Churchill, Hitler, and the Unnecessary War: How Britain Lost Its Empire and the West Lost the World*. New York: Crown, 2008.

Caidin, Martin. *Air Force: A Pictorial History of American Airpower*. New York: Bramhall House, 1957.

Caren, Eric C., ed. *Pearl Harbor Extra: A Newspaper Account of the United States' Entry into World War II*. Edison, N.J.: Castle Books, 2001.

Chambers, Whittaker. *Witness*. New York: Random House, 1952.

Chang, Iris. *The Rape of Nanking: The Forgotten Holocaust of World War II*. New York: Basic Books, 1997.

Choe, Wanne J. *Traditional Korea: A Cultural History*. Seoul: Hollym Publishing, 1997.

Cones, John W. *A Study in Motion Picture Propaganda: Hollywood's Preferred Movie Messages*. Marina Del Rey, Calif.: Rivas Canyon Press, 1998.

Connaughton, Richard. *Rising Sun and Tumbling Bear: Russia's War with Japan*. London: Cassell, 2004.

Cook, Fred J. *The Nightmare Decade: The Life and Times of Senator Joe McCarthy*. New York: Random House, 1971.

Coox, Alvin. *Nomohan: Japan against Russia, 1939*. Stanford: Stanford Univ. Press, 1985.

Costello, John. *Days of Infamy: Macarthur, Roosevelt, Churchill—The Shocking Truth Revealed*. New York: Simon & Schuster, 1994.

Courtois, Stéphane, et al. *The Black Book of Communism: Crimes, Terror, Repression*. Cambridge, Mass.: Harvard Univ. Press, 1999.

Craig, R. Bruce. *Treasonable Doubt: The Harry Dexter White Spy Case*. Lawrence, Kans.: Univ. of Kansas Press, 2004.

Cumings, Bruce. *Korea's Place in the Sun: A Modern History*, 2nd ed. New York: W. W. Norton, 1997.

———. *The Korean War: A History*. New York: Modern Library, 2010.

Davis, Kenneth S. *FDR: Into the Storm, 1937–1940*. New York: Random House, 1993.

———. *FDR: The War President, 1940–1945*. New York: Random House, 2000.

Dower, John W. *Embracing Defeat: Japan in the Wake of World War II*. New York: W. W. Norton, 1999.

Dray, Philip. *At the Hands of Persons Unknown: The Lynching of Black America*. New York: Random House, 2002.

Farr, Finis. *FDR*. New Rochelle, N.Y.: Arlington House, 1972.

Fehrenbach, T. R. *This Kind of War*. New York: Macmillan, 1963.

Feifer, George. *Breaking Open Japan: Commodore Perry, Lord Abe, and American Imperialism in 1853*. New York: Smithsonian Books / HarperCollins, 2006.

Fenby, Jonathan. *Chiang Kai-shek: China's Generalissimo and the Nation He Lost*. New York: Carroll & Graf, 2003.

Fischer, Louis. *Road to Yalta: Soviet Foreign Relations, 1941–1945*. New York: Harper & Row, 1972.

Fish, Hamilton. *FDR: The Other Side of the Coin*. New York: Vantage Press, 1976.

———. *Tragic Deception: FDR and America's Involvement in World War II.* Old Greenwich, Conn.: Devin Adair, 1983.

Fleming, Thomas. *The New Dealers' War: FDR and the War within World War II,* New York: Basic Books, 2001.

Gannon, Michael. *Pearl Harbor Betrayed: The True Story of a Man and a Nation under Attack.* New York: Henry Holt, 2001.

Garraty, John A., and Mark C. Carnes, eds. *American National Biography.* 24 vols. New York: Oxford Univ. Press, 1998.

Gluck, Carol, and Stephen R. Graubard, eds. *Showa: The Japan of Hirohito.* New York: W. W. Norton, 1990.

Goldstein, Donald M., Katherine V. Dillon, and J. Michael Wenger. *The Way It Was: Pearl Harbor.* New York: Brassey's, 1991.

Goodman, James. *Stories of Scottsboro.* New York: Pantheon, 1994.

Hack, Richard. *Puppetmaster: The Secret Life of J. Edgar Hoover.* Beverly Hills, Calif.: New Millenium Press, 2004.

Harries, Meirion, and Susie Harries. *Soldiers of the Sun: The Rise and Fall of the Imperial Japanese Army.* New York: Random House, 1992.

Hata, Ikuhiko. *The Nanking Atrocities.* Tokyo: Chisu Kuransha, 1986 (published in Japanese).

Haynes, John Earl, and Harvey Klehr. *Venona: Decoding Soviet Espionage in America.* New Haven: Yale Univ. Press, 1999.

Herman, Arthur. *Joseph McCarthy: Reexamining the Life and Legacy of America's Most Hated Senator.* New York: Free Press, 1999.

Hillier, J. *Japanese Colour Prints,* 3rd ed. London: Phaidon, 1998.

Hitler, Adolf. *Mein Kampf.* Translated by Ralph Manheim. Boston: Houghton Mifflin, 1942.

Houston, Jeanne Wakatsuki, and James D. Houston. *Farewell to Manzanar.* Boston: Houghton Mifflin, 1973.

Hu, Shizhang. *Stanley K. Hornbeck and the Open Door Policy, 1919–1937.* New York: Greenwood, 1995.

Jacobs, Benjamin, and Eugene Pool. *The 100-Year Secret: Britain's Hidden World War II Massacre.* Guilford, Conn.: Lyons Press, 2004.

Johnston, Stanley. *Queen of the Flat-Tops: The USS* Lexington *and the Coral Sea Battle*. New York: Dutton, 1942.

Kawahara, Toshiaki. *Hirohito and His Times: A Japanese Perspective*. New York: Kodansha, 1990.

Kawai, Kazuo. *Japan's American Interlude*. Chicago: Univ. of Chicago Press, 1960.

Kimmel, Husband E. *Admiral Kimmel's Story*. Chicago: Henry Regnery Co., 1955.

Kingman, Russ. *A Pictorial Life of Jack London*. New York: Crown, 1979.

Kinoaki, Matsuo. *How Japan Plans to Win*. Translated by Kilsoo Haan. Boston: Little, Brown, 1942.

Koster, Shizuko Obo. *Hachi-Ko: The Samurai Dog*. Frederick, Md.: PublishAmerica, 2007.

Kotani, Roland. *The Japanese in Hawaii: A Century of Struggle*. Honolulu: Hawaii Hochi, 1985.

Lamphere, Robert J., and Tom Schachtman. *The FBI-KGB War: A Special Agent's Story*, rev. ed. Macon, Ga.: Mercer Univ. Press, 1995.

Laqueur, Walter. *Stalin: The Glasnost Revelations*. New York: Scribner, 1990.

Layton, Edwin T. *And I Was There: Pearl Harbor and Midway—Breaking the Secrets*. New York: Morrow, 1985.

Link, Arthur S., ed. *The Papers of Woodrow Wilson*. Vol. 58, *April 23–May 9, 1919*. Princeton: Princeton Univ. Press, 1988.

Livingston, Jon, Joe Moore, and Felicia Oldfather, eds. *The Japan Reader*. 2 vols. New York: Pantheon, 1973.

London, Jack. *Jack London Reports*. Edited by King Hendricks and Irving Shepard. Garden City, N.Y.: Doubleday, 1970.

Lord, Walter. *Day of Infamy*. New York: Henry Holt & Co., 1957.

———. *Incredible Victory*. New York: Harper & Row, 1967.

Lukacs, John. *The Hitler of History*. New York: Knopf, 1997.

Machtan, Lothar. *The Hidden Hitler*. Translated by John Brownjohn. New York: Basic Books, 2001.

May, Gary. *Un-American Activities: The Trials of William Remington*. New York: Oxford Univ. Press, 1994.

Mayer, S. L., ed. *The Rise and Fall of Imperial Japan, 1894–1945*. London: Bison Books, 1976.

Meacham, Jon. *Franklin and Winston: An Intimate Portrait of an Epic Friendship*. New York: Random House, 2003.

Meeropol, Robert, and Michael Meeropol. *We Are Your Sons: The Legacy of Ethel and Julius Rosenberg*. Boston: Houghton Mifflin, 1975.

Meier, Andrew. *The Lost Spy: An American in Stalin's Secret Service*. New York: W. W. Norton, 2008.

Miller, Edward S. *War Plan Orange: The U.S. Strategy to Defeat Japan, 1897–1945*. Annapolis: Naval Institute Press, 1991.

Montefiore, Simon Sebag. *Young Stalin*. New York: Knopf, 2007.

Morgenthau, Henry, Sr. *Ambassador Morgenthau's Story*. New York: Doubleday, 1918. Reprint, New York: Cosimo, 2010.

Morley, James William. *The Japanese Thrust into Siberia, 1918*. New York: Columbia Univ. Press, 1957. Reprint, Whitefish, Mont.: Literary Licensing, 2011.

Mosley, Leonard. *Hirohito, Emperor of Japan*. Englewood Cliffs, N.J.: Prentice-Hall, 1966.

Musashi, Miyamoto. *The Book of Five Rings*, bilingual edition. Translated by William Scott Wilson. Tokyo: Kodansha, 2002.

Myer, Dillon S. *Uprooted Americans: The Japanese Americans and the War Relocation Authority during World War II*. Tucson: Univ. of Arizona Press, 1971.

Nitobe, Inazo. *Bushido: The Soul of Japan*, 10th revised and enlarged edition. New York: Putnam, 1907. Reprinted as *Bushido: The Samurai Spirit and the Soul of Japan*. Mineola, N.Y.: Dover, 2004.

Noma, Seiroku. *The Arts of Japan, Ancient and Medieval*. Translated by John Rosenfield. New York: Kodansha, 1966.

Oliver, Robert Tarbell. *A History of the Korean People in Modern Times, 1800 to the Present*. Newark: Univ. of Delaware Press, 1993.

———. *Syngman Rhee: The Man Behind the Myth*. New York: Dodd Mead, 1954.

Pavlov, Vitalii. *Operation Snow: Half a Century at KGB Foreign Intelligence*. Moscow: Gaia Herum, 1996 (published in Russian).

Pelta, Kathy. *The U.S. Navy*. Minneapolis: Lerner Publishing Group, 1990.

Perrin, Noel. *Giving Up the Gun: Japan's Reversion to the Sword, 1543–1879*. Boston: David R. Godine, 1990.

Popov, Dusko. *Spy/Counterspy*. New York: Grosset & Dunlap, 1974.

Powers, Richard Gid. *Secrecy and Power: The Life of J. Edgar Hoover*. New York: Free Press, 1987.

Prange, Gordon W. *At Dawn We Slept: The Untold Story of Pearl Harbor*. New York: McGraw-Hill, 1981.

———. *Pearl Harbor: The Verdict of History*. New York: McGraw-Hill, 1985.

———. *December 7, 1941: The Day the Japanese Attacked Pearl Harbor*: New York: McGraw-Hill, 1986.

Pringle, Heather. *The Master Plan: Himmler's Scholars and the Holocaust*. New York: Hyperion, 2006.

Rabe, John. *The Good Man of Nanking: The Diaries of John Rabe*. Translated by John E. Woods. New York: Knopf, 1998.

Radosh, Ronald, and Joyce Milton. *The Rosenberg File: A Search for the Truth*. New York: Holt, Rinehart & Winston, 1983.

Radzinsky, Edvard. *Stalin: The First In-Depth Biography Based on Explosive New Documents from Russia's Secret Archives*. Translated by H. T. Willetts. New York: Doubleday, 1996.

Rees, David. *Harry Dexter White: A Study in Paradox*. New York: Coward, McCann & Geoghegan, 1973.

Reeves, Thomas C. *The Life and Times of Joe McCarthy: A Biography*. New York: Stein & Day, 1982.

Reischauer, Edwin O. *Japan: The Story of a Nation*, 4th ed. New York: Knopf, 1991.

Reischauer, Haru Matsukata. *Samurai and Silk: A Japanese and American Heritage*. Cambridge, Mass.: Harvard Univ. Press, 1986.

Richardson, James O. *On the Treadmill to Pearl Harbor: The Memoirs of Admiral James O. Richardson*. Washington: U.S. Naval History Division, 1973.

Richie, Donald. *The Films of Akira Kurosawa*, 3rd ed. Berkeley: Univ. of California Press, 1991.

———. *The Japanese Movie: An Illustrated History*. Tokyo: Kodansha, 1966.

Roberson, John R. *Japan Meets the World: The Birth of a Superpower*. Brookfield, Conn.: Milbrook Press, 1998.

Romerstein, Herbert, and Eric Breindel. *The Venona Secrets: Exposing Soviet Espionage and America's Traitors*. Washington: Regnery 2000.

Rosenbaum, Ron. *Explaining Hitler: The Search for the Origins of His Evil*. New York: HarperCollins, 1998.

Ross, Ishbel. *An American Family: The Tafts, 1678 to 1964*. New York: World, 1964.

Russell, Francis. *Sacco & Vanzetti: The Case Resolved*. New York: Harper & Row, 1986.

Scammell, Michael. *Solzhenitsyn: A Biography*. New York: W. W. Norton, 1984.

Schecter, Jerrold, and Leona Schecter. *Sacred Secrets: How Soviet Intelligence Operations Changed American History*. Dulles, Va.: Brassey's, 2003.

Schlesinger Jr., Arthur M. *The Coming of the New Deal, 1933–1935*. Boston: Houghton Mifflin, 1958.

Scholl, Inge. *The White Rose: Munich, 1942–1943*. Translated by Arthur R. Schultz. Middletown, Conn.: Wesleyan Univ. Press, 1970.

Seagrave, Sterling. *The Soong Dynasty*. New York: Harper, 1986.

——— and Peggy Seagrave. *The Yamato Dynasty: The Secret History of Japan's Imperial Family*. New York: Broadway, 1999.

Seidensticker, Edward. *Low City, High City: Tokyo from Edo to the Earthquake*. New York: Knopf, 1983.

———. *Tokyo Rising: The City Since the Great Earthquake*. New York: Knopf, 1990.

Sherry. Michael S. *The Rise of American Air Power: The Creation of Armageddon*. New Haven: Yale Univ. Press, 1987.

Shirer, William L. *The Rise and Fall of the Third Reich: A History of Nazi Germany*. New York: Simon & Schuster, 1960.

Shiroyama, Saburo. *War Criminal: The Life and Death of Hirota Koki*. Translated by John Bester. New York: Kodansha, 1977.

Singer, Robert T. *Edo: Art in Japan 1615–1868*. Washington: National Gallery of Art, 1998.

Smythe, Lewis. *War Damage in the Nanking Area, December 1937 to March 1938: Urban and Rural Surveys*. Shanghai: Mercury Press, 1938.

Snow, Lois Wheeler. *Edgar Snow's China: A Personal Account of the Chinese Revolution Compiled from the Writings of Edgar Snow*. New York: Random House, 1981.

Spry-Leverton, Peter, and Peter Kornicki. *Japan*. New York: Facts on File, 1987.

Strachan, Hew. *The First World War*. New York: Oxford Univ. Press, 2001.

Sullivan, Robert, ed. *Our Call to Arms: The Attack on Pearl Harbor*. San Diego: Time-Life, 2001.

Summers, Anthony. *Official and Confidential: The Secret Life of J. Edgar Hoover*. New York: Putnam, 1993.

Tanaka, Masaaki. *What Really Happened in Nanking: The Refutation of a Common Myth*. Tokyo: Sekai Shuppan, 2000.

Tanaka, Yuki. *Hidden Horrors: Japanese War Crimes in World War II*. Boulder, Colo.: Westview Press, 1996.

Tateishi, John. *And Justice for All: An Oral History of the Japanese American Detention Camps*. New York: Random House, 1984.

Taylor, Theodore. *Air Raid—Pearl Harbor!* New York: Crowell, 1971.

Terasaki, Gwen. *Bridge to the Sun*. Chapel Hill: Univ. of North Carolina Press, 1957.

Theobald, Robert A. *The final secret of Pearl Harbor*. New York: Devin-Adair, 1954.

Theoharis, Athan G., and John Stuart Cox. *The Boss: J. Edgar Hoover and the Great American Inquisition*. Philadelphia: Temple Univ. Press, 1988.

Toland, John. *Infamy: Pearl Harbor and Its Aftermath*. Garden City, N.Y.: Doubleday, 1982.

———. *The Rising Sun: The Decline and Fall of the Japanese Empire, 1936–1945*. New York: Random House, 1970.

Tregaskis, Richard. *Guadalcanal Diary*. New York: Random House, 1943.

Underwood, Lillias Horton. *Fifteen Years among the Top-Knots, or Life in Korea*. New York: American Tract Society, 1904.

Van Der Vat, Dan. *Pearl Harbor: The Day of Infamy—An Illustrated History*. New York: Basic Books, 2001.

Wagenknecht, Edward. *The Seven Worlds of Theodore Roosevelt*, 2nd ed. Guilford, Conn.: Lyons Press, 2008.

Walder, David. *The Short Victorious War: The Russo-Japanese Conflict, 1904–1905*. New York: Harper & Row, 1973.

Warner, Denis, and Peggy Warner. *The Tide at Sunrise: A History of the Russo-Japanese War, 1904–1905*, 2nd ed. London: Routledge, 1974.

Weglyn, Michi. *Years of Infamy: The Untold Story of America's Concentration Camps*. New York: Morrow, 1976.

Weinstein, Allen. *Perjury: The Hiss-Chambers Case.* New York: Knopf, 1978.

———, and Alexander Vassiliev. *The Haunted Wood: Soviet Espionage in America—The Stalin Era.* New York: Random House, 1999.

Weintraub, Stanley. *Long Day's Journey into War: December 7, 1941.* New York: Truman Talley / Dutton, 1991.

Welles, Benjamin. *Sumner Welles: FDR's Global Strategist.* New York: St. Martin's, 1997.

Wels, Susan. *Pearl Harbor: America's Darkest Day.* San Diego: Time-Life, 2001.

White, G. Edward. *Alger Hiss's Looking-Glass Wars: The Covert Life of a Soviet Spy.* New York: Oxford Univ. Press, 2004.

White, Nathan. *Harry D. White—Loyal American.* Boston: B. W. Bloom, 1956.

Willmott, H. P. *Pearl Harbor.* London: Cassell, 2001.

Yamamoto, Masahiro. *Nanking : Anatomy of an Atrocity.* Westport, Conn.: Praeger, 2000.

Current Biography Yearbook: New York: H. W. Wilson Co, various years.

ARCHIVAL MATERIAL

Barnard College Archives: Intriguing Persons: Juliet Stuart Poyntz.

Bayerisches Hauptstaatsarchiv, "Hugo Gutmann" in *Deutsche jüdische Soldaten.* Munich.

The Charley Project, NYPD Missing Persons File, Juliet Stuart Poyntz.

Seeley G. Mudd Manuscript Library, Princeton, New Jersey, Harry Dexter White papers.

Smersh—Soviet Assassination Division of KGB (1917–), Archive.

MANUSCRIPTS

Ikuhiko Hata, "The Nanking Atrocities: Fact and Fable," from a seminar held at Princeton University on November 22, 1997, and article in *Shokun*, Japanese, printed in 1998.

Mitsuo Fuchida Memoirs, Japanese manuscript, private sources.

PERIODICALS

American Heritage. Pearl Harbor Anniversary Issue, December, 1991.

Barnard, Charles. "Back to Bataan." *Reader's Digest*, December 1980.

Bungei-Shunju (Japan) 85 (April 2007). Article on Matsuoka and Stalin.

Durdin, Frank. *New York Times*. Articles on Nanking, December 18, 1937, and December 22, 1937.

Fallows, James. "After Centuries of Japanese Isolation, a Fateful Meeting of East and West." *Smithsonian*, July, 1994: 20–32.

Japan, Asian-Pacific Perspectives (January 2007), "Educating the Future of Japan."

Lawless, Jill. "Apology for Kids Shipped from Britain." Associated Press, November 15, 2009.

Life. "Who Was Harry Dexter White?" November 23, 1953.

Saturday Evening Post. "How to Be a Crime Buster." March 19, 1955.

Time. "The Strange Case of Harry Dexter White." November 23, 1953.

Tresca, Carlo. "Where is Juliet Stuart Poyntz?" *Modern Monthly*, March 1939.

FILMS

Across the Pacific, directed by John Huston, screenplay by Richard Macaulay; from the *Saturday Evening Post* serial by Robert Carson; starring Humphrey Bogart, Mary Astor, Sydney Greenstreet, and Sen Yung, 1943.

Bataan, directed by Tay Garnett, screenplay by Robert D. Andrews; starring Robert Taylor, Thomas Mitchell, Lloyd Nolan and Robert Walker, 1943.

The Black Dragons, directed by William Nigh, screenplay by Harvey Gates; starring Bela Lugosi, Joan Barclay, and Clayton Moore., 1944.

Blood on the Sun, directed by Frank Lloyd, screenplay by Lester Cole and Nathaniel Curtis, story by Garrett Ford; starring James Cagney, Silvia Sydney, Wallace Ford, and Phillip Ahn, 1945.

Jack London, directed by Alfred Santell, screenplay by Ernest Pascal and Isaac Don Levine; starring Michael O'Shea, Susan Hayward, Virginia Mayo, and Ralph Morgan, 1943.

Pearl Harbor, directed by Michael Bay; starring Ben Affleck, Josh Harnett, Kate Beckinsale, and Cuba Gooding. 1991.

VIDEOS

Capra, Frank, *Why We Fight*, U.S. War Department.

Duncan, Dayton, *The National Parks: America's Best Idea*, a series by Ken Burns, 2009.

Isbouts, Jean-Pierre, *Operation Valkyrie: The Stauffenberg Plot to Kill Hitler*, Schwartz and Co.

Rees, Laurence, *Behind Closed Doors*, BBC.

Verklan, Laura, *Pearl Harbor*, The History Channel.

Williams, Sue, *The American Experience: Eleanor Roosevelt*, WGBH, Boston, 2000.

INTERVIEWS

Jon Allen, Southampton air raid survivor, later British officer.

Gene Anderson, U.S. Army, invasion of the Philippines, 1944–1945.

Len Cacutt, London firefighter, 1940–1941, RAF air gunner, 1941–1945.

Joseph Dorman, U.S. Army, Pearl Harbor survivor.

Bella Fellig, Holocaust fugitive from Austria to Switzerland.

Neil Finn, U.S. Navy medic with the Marines, Okinawa.

Thomas Vaughn Fitzgerald, U.S. Marines, Okinawa, Korea.

Herb Garelik, U.S. Army, Pearl Harbor and Guadalcanal survivor.

Helmut Hamaan, survivor of Hamburg air raid.

Joseph Horn, seven-year slave laborer, survivor of Auschwitz.

John Robert King, U.S. Marines, Bougainville, Okinawa, Korea, Vietnam.

Werner Koefler, survivor of Schweinfurt air raid.

Frank Kozar, U.S. Marines, Okinawa.

Takeo Obo, Japanese Imperial Navy, kamikaze pilot.

Shizuko Obo, survivor of air raids on Tokyo.

Leslie Potter, U.S. Army, Normandy, occupation of Germany.

Whitey Sefcik, U.S. Army, Saipan, 1944.

Nakayo Sotooka, survivor of air raids on Japan.

Arnold Steiner, U.S. Army, Bataan Death March survivor.

Harold Traber, U.S. Navy, Saipan, Philippines, Okinawa.

INDEX